Small Wonders

Small Wonders

Sermons for Children

Glen E. Rainsley

United Church Press

Cleveland, Ohio

Rosemary Laux

United Church Press, Cleveland, Ohio 44115
© 1998 by Glen E. Rainsley

From Archibald MacLeish, "Ars Poetica," reprinted from
Collected Poems by Archibald MacLeish, 1917–1952 by permission
of the Houghton Mifflin Company. Copyright 1926, 1954 by
Archibald MacLeish

Biblical quotations are from the New Revised Standard Version
of the Bible, © 1989 by the Division of Christian Education of the
National Council of the Churches of Christ in the U.S.A., and
are used by permission

Printed in the United States of America on acid-free paper

03 02 01 00 99 98   5 4 3 2 1

Library of Congress Cataloging-in-Publication Data
Rainsley, Glen E.
     Small wonders : sermons for children / Glen E. Rainsley.
          p.   cm.
     Includes index.
     ISBN 0-8298-1252-0 (pbk. : alk. paper)
     1. Children's sermons.   I. Title.
BV4315.R34   1998
252'.53—dc21   97-46837
                                                          CIP

6

To my daughter, Abby, source
of inspiration and brightness and insight

To my stepchildren, Laurie and Matthew
(now young adults), givers of breadth
and joy to family life

To all children, the story-tellers and
story-hearers who are skilled explorers
of God's Realm

9

Introduction

This book represents a new direction in writing for me. Having produced two volumes of prayers and liturgical resources for public worship or private devotions (*Words of Worship*, 1991; *Hear Our Prayer*, 1996; Pilgrim Press/United Church Press), my intent now is to provide engaging, creative, theologically solid materials for use with children. In a sense, this volume represents a return to my roots: not only was I once a child, but I also find consistently that the access route into God's realm is, as Jesus noted, discerned only by those with a childlike quality to their faith.

The contents of this book have been rigorously tested with children during my ministry to four congregations. All of the pieces have been "successful" to the extent that they have evoked and provoked lively responses, have led into good discussions, or have somehow proved memorable to participants. Knowing that children's lessons can also be met with blank stares, quizzical looks of befuddlement, or rambunctious behavior born of boredom, I offer these with a degree of confidence. Enjoy using them!

Why Include Children's Lessons/Sermons in Weekly Worship?

Including a children's lesson/sermon in congregational worship is hardly a liturgical necessity. Yet there are compelling reasons to do so. One parishioner stated with matter-of-fact forthrightness: "It's the one part of the service adults pay attention to and understand." Such a statement might seem a dagger in the heart of careful worship-planners, but it also contains more than a kernel of truth and identifies a seed of opportunity. In the section below, "What a Children's Lesson/Sermon Can Be," I will detail some of the opportunities to be realized. For now, I present just two more reasons for including such lessons/sermons, both of them deriving from basic faith beliefs.

First, we believe that Jesus valued children, welcoming them into his presence, healing them, identifying them as guides into God's realm. This attitude was entirely consistent with the whole of Jesus' topsy-turvy, countercultural message, for children in his day were prime examples of the least and lowly who easily could be ignored or demeaned. Jesus did not imply the pampering or hyperindulgence of children that can masquerade as caring among those with the means to pull it off. His concern, I think, was that we nurture the childlike qualities of curiosity and trustfulness, that we work toward creating a world fit for tomorrow's children. The children's lesson/sermon might be viewed as a tangible reminder of our call to pay attention to persons who get overlooked or set aside. Understood in this way, the lesson/sermon becomes a mission event, an act of doing justice, an affirmation of our resolve to practice Jesus' love in its entirety. By commending this approach and presenting it as a reason for including children's lessons/sermons in worship, I do not demand that everyone see it my way. My intent is much simpler, that of encouraging everyone who creates or presents a children's lesson/sermon to see it as a theologically purposeful activity.

Second, we believe that followers of Jesus Christ have a responsibility to foster the spiritual development of others in the faith family. That is a given of church life. It is also the promise we make to children when they get baptized. Our congregational words of welcome and support imply that there will be some intentional forms of follow-up. Placed in the context of sacramental activity and shared life, the children's lesson/sermon can be understood as one way in which the worshiping community fulfills its baptismal vows. The lesson/sermon demonstrates to children that the church takes seriously the communal task of Christian education. How reassuring, too, for children to see the church as a place where folks can be trusted to do what they say.

(How wonderful, too, if including a children's lesson/sermon were to inspire adults to assess or reassess how well we do what we say in all areas of church activity!)

What a Children's Lesson/Sermon Is Not

Although the temptation to do so is great, presenters should never use the lesson/sermon to exploit the cuteness factor of having children before an assembled congregation. Nor should the lesson/sermon have a design that draws attention to the cleverness of the presenter. Please note that I am not denying cuteness and not discouraging cleverness; I am saying that both of these can be serious distractions from the communication of a clear and meaningful message. Bottom line, a children's lesson/sermon is different from a performance and a congregation is different from an audience. Something has gone awry when congregants' dominant response is, "Weren't those kids adorable this morning," or, "Wasn't _____ ingenious to come up with that children's piece." Better that congregants experience the lesson/sermon as a time of spirited closeness with the church's children, as a memorable message enhancing their understanding of God. Will the children be entrancing on a regular basis? Yes, but that is not the point. Will presenters come up with commendably creative offerings? Yes, but that is not the point, either. And even as we express gratitude for the gifts of children and presenters, we must be diligent in developing a hunger for God that is not dependent for satisfaction on cuteness or cleverness.

The lesson/sermon is never a proper time to put children on the spot. Such an experience can be devastating to a child. It may produce a few laughs among observers, especially those who suffer from the disease of enjoying the anguish of others, but the cost is likely to be an increase of anxiety among the children. Many years ago, a minister who was hoping to get a list of names useful in personalizing his talk about forgiveness, asked the children gathered before him, "Tell me who it is who annoys you." The children froze. It sounded to them as though anyone they named might be in for punishment. The clergyman persisted. "Come now," he said sharply, "there must be someone who annoys you." Again, dead silence until a first-grader who wanted to help the situation blurted out, "You." That was an on-target response, an honest reaction to being placed on the spot.

The lesson/sermon is not the proper occasion for presenting material that requires immediate and thorough discussion (unless church school or some other setting provides a forum for dealing with issues raised). The children's lesson/sermon, if set within a worship service, is necessarily time-limited. Further, the highly visible and public environment may inhibit the kinds of questioning or voiced reflection that are most needed. It is, to my mind, best to keep the tone of a children's lesson/sermon one that inspires responses brightly conversational rather than deeply dialogical. A caution: If discussion-prompting topics do get presented in a discussion-inhibiting context, the message to children is clear. They will identify the lesson/sermon as a lecture or pronouncement, and they will begin to perceive genuine give-and-take as a rarity or as something discouraged in the church environment.

Finally, the children's lesson/sermon is not the time to reiterate the same message on a weekly basis. I have sat through countless presentations which state: "You're special because God loves you," or, "It's so special that God loves you." I do not want to debate the importance of communicating those two points, and I do realize the role of repetition in educating small children. However . . . children possess the capability to grasp quite a range of theological concepts, and they possess the capability of getting bored with sameness. We owe it to children to give them a breadth of spiritual input and experience. Another caution: Monitor and severely limit use of the word "special" in children's lessons/sermons.

What a Children's Lesson/Sermon Can Be

Above all else, a children's lesson/sermon can be a primary connecting point with the church community. It gives children an opportunity, in the most relaxed portion of a worship service, to relate with adults in the church family. And the basic message of any children's lesson/sermon, conveyed no matter what the content, is a relational message: We need one another if we are to make progress toward our common goal of faith development.

The lesson/sermon can be a means for introducing and exploring some of the key resources that nurture our faith development—stories from scripture, theological concepts, liturgical traditions and significant holidays, contemporary examples of enacted belief, images of God in daily life. As children gain awareness of and access to these resources, they will have reinforced an instinctive childhood understanding of faith as all-encompassing. To the extent that children's lessons/sermons help build up such an understanding, they have an impact that is spiritually instructive and productive. Using a variety of genres amplifies the message that no aspect of human activity is exempt from faith considerations; we will look at how to build variety into children's lessons/sermons in the section below, "Genres and Techniques."

A lesson/sermon can be a meaningful worship experience. It is usually that portion of a Sunday service most specifically designed to draw in children. As they participate in it, engaging their spirits in an explicitly God-revealing and God-celebrating event, the lesson/sermon truly becomes liturgy (literally, "the work of the people"). I lobby hard for high-quality lessons/sermons and enthusiastic presentation because a child's positive response to worship opens a bit wider the doors leading to future faithfulness. Would it not be wonderful indeed to raise up a generation which felt steadfast gladness at going to the house of God (see Psalm 122)? Excellent children's lessons/sermons may be a small but significant step in that direction.

We must keep in the very front of our adult minds a simple recognition of the fact that lessons/sermons we create *for* children offer a prime opportunity for us to learn *from* them. If the lessons/sermons are at all interactive, there is no question we will learn from children. From their naivete and their wisdom. From their desire to believe and their capacity to doubt. From their silence and their laughter. From their blunt queries and their profound observations. From their intentions and their actions. We will glimpse God through children and we will see ourselves more clearly. We will be reminded, again, how we need one another in order to develop in faith.

A final note. A lesson/sermon succeeds if it conveys to children a potent message worthy of weekly repetition: "You are part of the church family. You are listeners to and interpreters of the good news."

Genres and Techniques

In presenting children's lessons/sermons, variety in format is essential. No single genre or technique will consistently encourage curiosity, evoke questions, and enhance retention. Although variety serves a vital anti-boredom function, I am not advocating variety solely for that reason. Stated bluntly, the richness of the message we have to share with children cannot adequately find expression through one format. Some Bible stories lend themselves to dramatization, some take on life when introduced through puzzles or games. Object lessons open up understandings of certain concepts, while straightforward personal stories convey other insights. Good communication requires that we select a genre and a presentational style that best suit the theme or topic of the lesson/sermon. This takes a hefty amount of creative thinking and analysis. A perusal of the Gospels shows us, should we need inspiration to put in the effort such a thought process demands, that Jesus used a wide variety of teaching techniques. In terms of genres, he used parable and sermon and dialogue and quotation from scripture. He taught by means of personal example and enactment of God's power and object lesson. He got his message across. If we hope to do the same, children's lessons/sermons merit a conscientious exercise of Christly creativity.

Using a variety of genres and techniques also makes a statement about the church's desire to be inclusive. Research into how people learn indicates clearly that we absorb information/concepts/data in numerous ways. Some folks learn best by listening. Others are visual learners. Some need to follow a sequence. Others readily process random materials. Some have a tactile approach to learning. Others learn by taking free flights of imagination. As effectively as we can, we should use the variety of genres and techniques available to us so that people will receive what we offer in ways they can best understand. A disciplined commitment to variety in children's lessons/sermons makes a subtle yet earnest statement about inclusiveness, and also about the importance of that which is being shared.

Some Forms of Children's Lessons/Sermons

There are countless forms that a children's lesson/sermon may take. I note below a few of these, along with brief comments and cautions.

1. Straight story or parable—Probably from the days of cave dwellers on, storytellers have served as conveyors of ideas and beliefs. A well-crafted story, delivered with full personal investment on the part of the presenter, can communicate just about any message in a way that is virtually indelible upon the memory. The Christian gospel, in its earliest form, seems to have been passed along as powerful stories describing Jesus' ministry, message, death, and resurrection. And Jesus' own teaching used that challenging literary form called the parable to help folks sharpen their spiritual discernment. Stories and parables have played key roles in our faith history, and children's affinity for them suggests that they should be a staple of the Christian education diet.

2. Object lesson—The basic purpose of any object lesson is to make the verbal visual, thereby providing another point of reference for listeners. The task of creating a meaningful object lesson is similar to that of creating a poem—namely, the task of finding the right metaphor. Archibald MacLeish concludes his poem "Ars Poetica" with the lines "A poem should not mean/But be." An object lesson, at its best, also should not mean, but be. If that sounds convoluted or weird, consider how often and how easily we use metaphors or object lessons in precisely this way: Shelter to the homeless *is* the love of God. A church with doors open to all *is* a holy community. The cross *is* salvation. Christ *is* present in the sharing of bread and cup.

An object lesson carefully constructed and well presented lingers in the memory, often enabling faith to be experienced in serendipitous ways. A parishioner stopped by my office one afternoon to say, "The other day when I grabbed my tennis racquet to play, I started thinking about how I might use my talents at the church." My own racquet having been the featured object of the previous Sunday's lesson, I replied, "Great! I'm glad you listened to the children's sermon. So let's get together on the court soon and we can talk about what you're wanting to offer." (The tennis racquet lesson/sermon is included in this book.) Another parishioner grabbed me by the arm during a fellowship hour. He said, "I'm in New York last Wednesday having a business lunch with a client. We're at a Chinese restaurant, and we've wrapped up our deal, so we're just eating and schmoozing. And all of a sudden as I'm using my chopsticks, I think of another way they tell us about our faith, one you didn't mention in the children's sermon. I just stop talking for a few seconds so I can think on it and the client thinks I've gone into brain-lock. It worked out okay but it was embarrassing. Next time we do Italian." (The chopstick lesson/sermon is also in this book.)

Those two comments reveal one of the positive features of object lessons. They invite feedback. At the time of presentation, objects serve as focal points for attention as well as starting points for directed dialogue. For surprising lengths of time after a lesson, contact with the object(s) used may trigger theological questions or inspire insights or lead to further conversation.

3. High-participation activities—Many scripture stories or faith themes lend themselves to being used in ways requiring much involvement on the part of children. Sometimes, as with spontaneously casted dramas, the participation is on-the-spot, yet rather carefully choreographed and scripted. (There are a couple of examples in this book.) A fill-in format that elicits responses from children also has the feel of immediacy, though within the bounds of a set text. Truly impromptu conversations with children also certainly have a place within the spectrum of effective lesson/sermon forms. These should be thought out carefully by the presenter in terms of how questions get phrased, what topics suit such a loose structure, and whether or not another method may be better.

As a long-time improvisational actor, I have come to cherish the creative energy of "the moment." As a pastor, I pass along a simple caution: When the uninhibitedness of children is coupled with the safety we hope they feel in a church setting, we may find the truths they voice (a good thing!) out of context in the worship setting (a sensitive situation). I offer two examples from my own experience. Wishing to make a point about God's capacity to help us deal with wrongdoing, I asked the assembled children, "What sorts of things do you think of as really wrong?" Three responses into the lesson/sermon, a boy blurted out, "My big brother sneaking out with the car last week." Instant family issue. Instant wider issue, since big brother's girlfriend accompanied him. Instant legal issue, since big brother was not old enough to possess a driver's license. On another occasion, the theme being hopes and dreams, I cheerily asked the children, "What do you most wish for?" A girl responded quickly in a tone of fervent sadness, "I wish Daddy would stop hitting Mommy." To say that the subsequent seconds of silence were painful would be a gross understatement. That was pastorally important information, though clearly presented in a less than ideal venue. Open, free conversation with children has its place within the lesson/sermon setting. It does, however, require careful planning and a willingness to deal with responses that range from silliness to unnerving forthrightness.

4. Lesson/sermon presented by children—It is important for children to have times of sharing with the congregation in a very direct way. Some church school curricula make provision for such opportunities on a regular basis. And church, to my mind, can benefit from lessons/sermons presented by children. These presentations serve to educate congregants about the content of church school sessions (through dramas, narratives, project or poster displays, etc.) or about the outreach efforts of children (participation in hunger or child sponsorship projects, creation of AIDS quilts, local mission involvements, etc.). The presentations may also take the form of worship-enhancing contributions (banners or music, for example). There is no question that congre-

gants hear messages of faith in a new way, often a profoundly compelling way, when they are delivered by children.

5. Laity-presented lesson/sermon—Any form of children's lesson/sermon may be offered by a layperson. The contents of this book are absolutely "laity-friendly." It needs to be said that a significant message conveyed to children through laity-presented lessons/sermons is a consistent one—that the church, as a community, abounds with people who have stories of faith to share. The crucial submessage: Faith is common property, not something clergy alone profess, practice, and dole out.

An essential for church life is the establishment of a mechanism for encouraging lay participation in children's lessons/sermons and for working with persons who come forth. Invitations from the pulpit, idea boxes, newsletter beckonings and contests are all tried-and-true means of prompting involvement. The process of working with volunteers requires caring, careful attention. Personally, I believe that a pastor should be the primary contact. The process affords a fine opportunity for theological dialogue with a congregant, for creative planning and/or problem-solving, and for expressing gratitude to someone investing his or her talent in the church's children.

6. Liturgy produced and presented by children—One of the greatest Christian learning experiences a child can have is that of producing and presenting the liturgy for a Sunday worship service. Even young children can shape benedictions or prayers of dedication. Third through fifth graders may be assigned calls to worship or prayers of thanksgiving. Sixth through eighth graders are often skilled crafters of prayers of confession, words of assurance, or introductions to silent prayer. Pastoral prayers sometimes take form as a collective effort, a collage of group concerns. Sermons emerge from children of every age!

Obvious though the point may be, I want to stress how helpful it is for children to get a feel for the way each liturgical component contributes to the whole worship event. A review of Sunday bulletins provides the most straightforward method of explaining the format, sequence, and elements of worship. My two previous books (*Words of Worship* and *Hear Our Prayer*) also offer useful explanatory material.

The keys to having a positive experience with children's ventures into liturgy are these: preparation and practice. When children prepare thoughtfully and possess a sense of the high purpose of their work, their faith can truly find its voice. And what they have to say is often surprising or touching or refreshing or challenging or a moving mixture of all these combined. When children practice their presentation, they not only gain valuable speaking skills, but also assure that their message will get heard. When serious effort is given to preparation and practice, the downside to a service produced and presented by children is minimal. And the upside potential is limited only by the extent of God's grace.

Use of This Book

Most of the lessons/sermons you will find in this book are ready-to-go in their present form. Each one lists required materials, offers samples of needed illustrations, and provides a complete text. Some of the lessons/sermons serve more as models to be revised, expanded, or adapted to fit specific congregational settings. All may be used with small or large groups of children. All benefit from having the text owned and personalized by the presenter.

I have loosely arranged the lessons/sermons to allow for easy access, and I have tagged each one with a specific theme (or, in some cases, two or three). There are a few pieces designed for special occasions, for example, a mission Sunday or the start of church school. Several pertain to holidays or liturgical seasons. A good number relate to basic faith concepts and outreach issues. The simple index will guide you to the items most helpful for specific needs.

I hope these lessons/sermons find much use as resources that aid presenters and provide children with materials both challenging and enjoyable. I hope, too, that this book serves to inspire its users toward creating excellent new lessons/sermons for the children who, with us, seek the fullness of life in God's realm.

Small Wonders

Advent

Since we are now in the season of Advent, I thought it would be a good idea to check out your knowledge of the story we will be hearing on Christmas. Do you think you know what happened pretty well? I am going to read you a version of the Christmas story, but I believe there are some mistakes in it. In fact, I am quite certain there are exactly eight mistakes. As soon as you hear a mistake and know how to correct it, raise your hand. Ready?

[*Note:* Mistakes to be read are contained in parentheses; corrections are bracketed. It is important for the reader not to slow down or stop at the mistakes. Read through them until there are several hands in the air.]

It came to pass in those days that Caesar Augustus wanted all the world to be taxed. So Joseph and his wife (Laverne) [Mary] left the village of Nazareth to journey to the city of David which is called (Boston)* [Bethlehem]. While they were in Bethlehem it came time for Mary to give birth to her child. Because there was no room (at the Holiday Inn, they went to a run-down motel) [at the inn, they went to spend the night in the stable]. There Mary's first child was born. She took him and laid him in a manger while all the animals—(alligators, rhinoceroses, kangaroos) [sheep, cattle, donkeys]—looked on.

In the fields around Bethlehem there were shepherds watching their flocks by night. And as they looked up, (an enormous golden stork) [an angel of the Lord] appeared to them and told them the good and joyous news of the baby's birth. "A Saviour

---

*The name of any nearby city may be used.

3

has been born to you who is the Messiah." Suddenly there were many angels praising God and singing (Happy Birthday to Jesus, Happy Birthday . . .) [Glory to God in the highest and on earth peace, good will to all]. So the shepherds hurried off to see the baby and then told all their friends about him.

Later, from far away, (basketball players from the Orlando Magic) [Magi from the East] began a journey to find the baby. A bright star guided them as they traveled. Finally, they (pulled off the interstate at the Bethlehem exit, parked their motorcycles . . .) [arrived at Bethlehem and found Mary and the baby]. Immediately they worshiped him, and after unloading their camels, offered him gifts of gold and frankincense and myrrh.

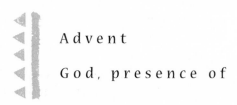

Advent

God, presence of

Preparation: Sing "What Child Is This?" (full congregation or with children)

The song we just sang asks the question, "What Child Is This?" Then it goes on to tell us some things about the child who, it turns out, is both "the Christ" and "the babe, the son of Mary." This child has become someone very important in my life for a particular reason. Let me tell you about it.

When I was very young, I had the feeling that I did not understand God much at all.

Sometimes people described God to me in ways that caused me to picture God as a sort of old man in a white beard who looked very kind at times and very angry at others. God lived "up there" somewhere way beyond the stars in a place called heaven. That faraway God was so distant from me that I could not get close enough to gain an understanding.

Then sometimes I thought that it was God who made the thunder thunder and the windows rattle and the house go creak-and-groan when I was home by myself. That noisy-scary God I did not want to understand because I was too frightened.

Then someone told me that God was everywhere. So I searched for God under the sofa, in the middle of big clumps of bushes, and on top of closet shelves where old clothes and miscellaneous stuff got stored. I poked around in all sorts of good places. But I never quite found God. I certainly could not understand this hide-and-seek God who always seemed not to be wherever I looked.

Finally, I remember learning about what Christmas really means. When I found out that God came to be with us as a person named Jesus, I recall feeling glad, because a person was someone I could learn to know and to understand. It was comforting and exciting to think of Jesus as someone who started as a baby just as we do, to think of him as someone who sensed the world and experienced feelings. What was best of all and most satisfying of all, though, was when I came to realize that because God lived as a person, God truly understands us in every possible way. During Advent, that is something I celebrate especially—God understands us.

Each Sunday of Advent we will be lighting a candle to prepare for the birthday of the One who *is* the child we sang about, the Christ child who gives us our deepest understanding of God. [Candle-lighting may follow.]

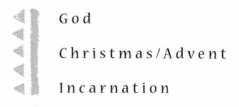

God

Christmas/Advent

Incarnation

Materials: A tube sock, eyes made out of felt, a nose (a table tennis ball is perfect), felt or cloth ears, tabs of Velcro*

I would like to try a thinking game with you today. When I say the name of an animal, I want you to think hard and to picture that animal in your mind. Ready? A horse . . . A lion . . . A whale . . . A zebra . . . A griblyk.

You cannot do that last one, can you? Even if you do imagine what a griblyk looks like, we cannot be sure we are all imagining the same kind of animal. It just so happens that I am quite sure I am the only one here who knows what a griblyk looks like. But I really want you all to know, too. So I will show you the best way I can.

- A griblyk has a body like this. [put sock over hand]
- A griblyk has a big mouth like this. [poke a deep mouth into the sock and begin to work mouth]
- A griblyk has eyes just like these. [attach eyes and have creature look around]
- A griblyk has a nose much larger than you might expect. [affix table tennis ball and have creature sniff about]
- A griblyk has ears that hear the softest sounds. [attach ears and have creature listen attentively]
- Griblyks are smart, too. [have creature address a child by name]

*Small pieces of Velcro will serve well as the means of attaching eyes, nose and ears to the griblyk. These pieces and the sock should, of course, be prepared ahead.

That is a griblyk. So now, if I ever ask you again to picture one in your mind, you will know what to think about, for you have seen what a griblyk looks like and you know a bit about how one acts.

It is not particularly important that people know everything (or anything!) about griblyks. But it is very important that people know what God is like, how God acts. This time before Christmas that we call Advent is an especially happy time for us because we celebrate the coming into this world of a person who puts a face to God, a person whose birthday we know as the holy day of Christmas. This is also the time of year when we seem to care most for each other, to enjoy life most, to understand best what God expects from us. This all fits together. When Jesus was born, God was saying, "By knowing this person Jesus, you will know me." We look at what Jesus did, how he acted with other people, what he said and how he said it, and we begin to see/understand God. Put another way: If we want to know what God is like, what God hopes for us, we need to learn about Jesus. And as we do, we will sense truly and deeply why this time of year is a season of brightness, joy, and caring.

[A candle-lighting service may follow.]

New Year Gifts

Materials: a toy, a piece of sports equipment, an article of clothing, a book, a tape or CD, an item of food (preferably a dessert)

Since the last time we met together during the worship service, many of us have received gifts. Most of these gifts came to us as part of our celebration of Jesus' birthday. There are all sorts of gifts that people get, and they are used in a whole variety of ways. I have brought with me a few kinds of gifts.

1. [Show toy and piece of sports equipment] Gifts such as these we use for play. They provide us with opportunities for enjoyment, recreation, and exercise. A musical instrument would be another example of a gift meant for play.

2. [Show article of clothing] A clothing gift gets worn. We might use it for protection (from the cold or while taking part in an outdoor activity) or for certain occasions (for school or for sports or for sleeping).

3. [Show book] We read books that come to us as gifts. We use them to learn about our world and to help our imaginations grow.

4. [Show tape or CD] We listen to these gifts. We use them to brighten our lives, to enlarge our appreciation of music, to help us feel.

5. [Show food item] We gobble up food gifts. We use them to help us grow in body and, sometimes, just to savor the flavor.

One gift more we have all received recently. [Name the day of the week for New Year's Day.] In addition to all the other new things I mentioned, we have been offered by God the gift of a *new year;* this one is called *(19__/20__)*. It is up to us to decide how we are going to use it. Probably the best way of using *(19__/20__)* is to do some specific things/projects/activities that serve to say thank-you to God for giving us the new year as a gift. I would like you to think about what a couple of those things might be. Talk to a teacher or to a parent or to me. Then write down your ways of using this year in a way that thanks God for giving it. Whatever you choose, let it be your promise to God.

To use any gift well is the very best thanks we can offer.

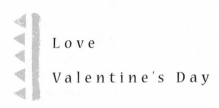

Love

Valentine's Day

When I was in elementary school, this time of year was exciting to me because of three things that would be happening during the couple of months ahead: Valentine's Day, my birthday, and the start of baseball season. [*Note:* The second and third items should be personalized to fit the presenter of this lesson. Some common possibilities might be the coming of spring, a week's school vacation, etc.] It is the first of those I want to talk about with you for a few minutes.

I remember that for a couple of weeks before Valentine's Day, I would be hard at work punching cards out of sheets and tucking them into envelopes that I had decorated with fancy designs. Or I would use colored paper, doilies, yarn, markers, felt, and ribbon to make elaborate cards that did not fit into any envelope. What

was wonderful about the holiday—what felt good and joyous—
was that after signing zillions of cards, "Love from _____
(name of presenter)," I would send them off to everybody. Parents,
neighbors, sisters, brothers, grandparents, teachers and classmates, aunts and uncles, mail carrier and minister. And all of them
were glad to receive the cards.

Then in junior high and senior high school, there came a time
when it was not cool to send lots of cards. Valentine's Day got
very serious. Giving a card to someone meant that everyone
would think you "liked" that person, and in a few days the talk
around school would practically have you married. So my "Love
from _____ (name of presenter)" did not get written on
cards for years and years. As a grown-up, I started sending cards
again to my family, mostly to children, but also to others.

I enjoy sending the cards, so it feels better now. But there is
something inside me that misses sending Valentine's Day cards to
everyone. I believe that one of the qualities Jesus most appreciated and valued in children was an openness to saying, "I love
you," to all sorts of folks. And I know that if God were to send
Valentine's Day cards, every single person in the world would get
one. No one would be left out. That is just the way God's love is
every day, and it is how God hopes ours will be. Bright. Joyous.
Inspired. Inclusive. So enjoy getting ready for Valentine's Day
over the weeks ahead, and let it remind you that God's love in-
cludes you—everyone.

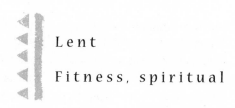

Lent

Fitness, spiritual

Materials: An unfolded box (a gift box or bakery box with a lid that works well), an assembled/folded version of the same box

I am going to show you a couple of objects and I would like you to tell me what they are.

[Show unfolded box and lid] What is this? [responses]

I guess we could say it is a box that is not yet a box.

[Show assembled/folded box and lid] What is this? [responses]

This is a box.

The first object I showed you is not all that useful. About the only things I could think of using it for were these: to cover over a hole in a broken window, to make a not very pretty sign, to shred as a fire-starter, to use as an awkward kind of giant fly-swatter. The second object I showed you is very useful. The box can be used for storing all sorts of stuff or for carrying it around. And if you had about four hundred of these boxes you could build a terrific castle.

Do any of you like to play or to watch sports? [brief responses or show of hands] In order to be good at sports, one of the most important things you have to accomplish is to get in shape. That means having your body ready to do all it can do. The problem with the first box I showed you is that it was out of shape; it could not do what a box is supposed to do. It needed to "shape up," something we get told to do by various people throughout our lives.

It is healthy for us to get in shape. That is true for us physically and it is true for us spiritually. Here in church, one of the things we try to help one another do is to get in shape with our faith, to shape up our lives as we believe God wants them shaped. We pay particular attention to this during the season of Lent. The more we work on this, the more we help one another, the more useful we are. What I mean by that is this: we become spiritually fit, and so become able to store God's love within us, to carry it all over the place, to open ourselves up [open box] so we can pour it out.

Faith

Lent

Materials: A pair of chopsticks

The more we learn about our faith, the more we understand that God is everywhere in our lives. And that makes us look at the world, other people, and ourselves from a new and exciting point of view.

Sometimes we get taught about our faith in ways that amaze us. I look at all sorts of things and find that God has something to say through just about everything around me. Last week while eating fried rice and grabbing for wontons in a plate of soup, I discovered that these items [show chopsticks] reminded me of how we are to live as people faithful to God.

How so?

1. They remind me that faith requires patience. Sometimes when I use a spoon or fork, the utensils tend to serve as shovels.

Being hungry can make me race through food—a one-minute bowl of cereal, a two-minute piece of pie, a meal that seems like a sprint. Chopsticks get me to slow down on the food I eat with them, to take smaller bites, to be more at ease. We need to do that with our faith, to realize we should not rush through worship or prayer or study, to see that we can take our time (a whole lifetime) to get faith's flavor.

2. Chopsticks remind me that faith holds surprises. When I first tried to use them, I never thought I would get them to work—and I was surprised as could be when, after a bit of practice, they did. The more we get involved with God, the more we find our faith to be surprising. We learn astonishing things: that God hears prayers, that we really can make a difference in the world, that church can be the most joyful place in our lives.

3. Chopsticks remind me that faith calls us to mission. I cannot eat with these without thinking of people half a world away; whenever I use them, I am eating food from China or Southeast Asia. The foods we consider common in North America are not made to be eaten with chopsticks (for example, chopsticks do not work well on hot dogs or hamburgers or chocolate cake). Our faith tells us what the chopsticks tell us—that we need to think beyond ourselves, always keeping in mind that no matter where people are, they are part of God's family and they are welcome at Christ's table.

4. Chopsticks remind me that faith pulls us together into a community, into a church. Chopsticks do not work unless they make contact with one another (stabbing food with one is not too effective). People of faith also need contact with one another to learn and to serve God together. We are not meant to go it alone. We need each other as much as one chopstick needs its partner.

The season coming up, Lent, is a time to focus on our faith, to sense God's presence all through our lives. Perhaps it is even a time to listen to chopsticks.

Lent

Mission

Materials: A dinner plate with the following items on it—a tablespoon of dried milk, a tablespoon of sugar, a hard-boiled egg, a carrot, a potato, a tablespoon of raisin and dried apple, a slice of bread, a dime and five pennies (or a nickel)

How much do you think it costs to feed you each day? [responses] Let me check with parents now to see what they figure it costs. [responses]

For many, many of the world's people, the amount of money they have to buy their food for a day is approximately equal to this [hold out a dime and five pennies]. That's it—fifteen cents.

If that does not seem like much to you, perhaps your reaction is exactly correct. It is *not* much. Let me show you what you might be able to get for fifteen cents. I have put together a plateful of foods familiar to you. [Bring out plate with items on it. Point to each as you identify them.]

Tablespoon of dried milk—½¢
Tablespoon of sugar—½¢
Egg—7¢
Carrot—4¢
Potato—3¢
Tablespoon of raisin and dried apple—6¢
Slice of bread—4¢

Oops. All together, these things cost about twenty-five cents, so if you had just fifteen cents to spend, you could eat only some of them as all your food for a whole day. How do you think you would feel after a couple of weeks or months of a diet like this?

[responses] Do you think you could work or play much? [responses] Would you want someone you love to have to live on fifteen cents a day? [responses]

Life on fifteen cents a day is a hard life, not a healthy life, probably a short life. We do, however, have ways of helping people who are hungry. And we have Jesus' teaching, the example of the early church, and the words of a biblical letter-writer named John all urging us to feed the hungry as a clear way of showing that God's love is at work in us and through us. For those with little, let's put food on their plates.

[*Note:* This lesson provides a fitting introduction to mission-giving programs (Heifer Project; One Great Hour of Sharing; CROP; Bread for the World, or denominational hunger relief efforts; or child sponsorship). The plate makes a fine fellowship hour display encouraging donations targeted at addressing hunger concerns. During Lent, there may be persons in the congregation who wish to follow the fifteen-cent diet for one or more days per week.]

Palm Sunday
Faith

Materials: Some palm leaves, a palm plant

What kind of leaf is this? [show leaf] What sort of plant is that on the floor? [responses] What special day is today? Hold up your hand and show me your palm if you know the answer! (Palm Sunday)

When Jesus entered the city of Jerusalem long ago, people tore down palm branches and spread them before him as he rode a donkey along the road. Folks did that to welcome and to honor Jesus—the palms were used as decorations for his path. For much of the time since then, palm leaves have been used in celebrating this Sunday; they are reminders of what happened when Jesus entered Jerusalem.

I think that if we have the palm plant as a symbol of our faith, it is good to know that there is more to the palm than decoration. It is truly one of the most useful plants you can imagine.

Some palms produce dates and can also be a source of sugar. Other palms produce coconuts—from these you can get coconut oil and coconut milk and the nutmeat itself, which can be eaten as is or cooked or dried (and put into more interesting things like custard pies).

The husk of the coconut has a fiber called coir (pronounced: kyar) that is used to make a strong rope.

The wood and leaves of the palm tree are used by millions of people in the building of their houses or shelters.

If you can remember these things about the palm, they can remind you what our faith does for us, too: like food, faith nourishes us in spirit to help us grow into stronger people; like rope, faith gives us something to hold on to or to hold things together in tough times; like wood and leaves, faith provides our hearts and minds and spirits with a place to call home. Palms can be decoration, and much more. Faith can be decoration—and also, much more.

Palm Sunday

Materials: A conductor's baton or a foot-long piece of dowel

I have always wanted to try being a conductor, but that is rather hard to do without having a music group to conduct, a choir or a band or an orchestra. Last week, though, I came up with an idea for something we can do together this morning. I am going to conduct a story, and you are going to be the sounds. The story is the exciting one of Palm Sunday. It has six sound-parts we will need you to produce.

[At this time, divide children into six groups numbered 1 through 6; if there are not enough children to have at least three per group, use the congregation and/or choir to take the parts of "crowd," "city," or "enemies." The groups should be arranged so that they can be pointed to individually by the "conductor's baton."]

Here are the sounds I want you to make when I point to you with the baton. And please stop making the sound when I pull back the baton.

1. Friends of Jesus—Whistle a little tune or a single note; hum if you cannot whistle
2. Crowd—Say hosanna, hosanna, hosanna
3. Palms—Say swish, swish, swish
4. Donkey—Say clip-clop, clip-clop
5. City—Say hubbub, hubbub, hubbub
6. Enemies of Jesus—Say mutter, mutter, mutter

Here we go!

One day while Jesus was in Bethphage near the Mount of Olives, he turned to his friends (1), his disciples, and said to them, "It is time to go to Jerusalem." "But Jesus," they replied, "if you enter that city (5) your enemies (6) will try to kill you." Jesus had made up his mind, however. He gave directions to two of the disciples to go into a village to obtain a donkey (4) for him to ride. So off went the disciples. In the village, they found the animal tied. When they began to untie it, the owner said, "What are you doing?" The disciples answered, "My friend (1) Jesus has need of it and will return it to you." Soon the disciples came back to Jesus leading the donkey (4), which no one had ever ridden.

Quickly, Jesus' followers put some of their clothes upon the little animal's back, and then Jesus climbed on. All set off toward the city (5). As Jesus rode along on the donkey (4), people came out to welcome him with shouts and waves. A noisy crowd (2) lined the road. Some of them tore down branches of palms (3) to lay before the donkey (4) as it passed. "Blessed be the One who comes in the name of God!" they shouted. The crowd (2) followed Jesus and waved palms (3) as he traveled toward the city (5) where he would spend one final week with his friends (1) and where he would die at the hands of his enemies (6).

Thank you for your help in telling the story!
[Closing comments may be offered.]

Holy Week

Materials: A poster board containing the eight punctuation marks arranged as in Figure 1 (Figure 2 illustrates how the board will appear at the end of the lesson); a marking pen. A tripod or easel to hold the poster board is helpful.

I have a poster board to show you. After we work with it a bit, it will help you learn or remember the story of Holy Week. [Show poster board with eight punctuation marks written on it.] What you see is eight different punctuation marks. We will connect them with the story of Holy Week and turn them into pictures to describe events and make meanings memorable. Let's go through the week.

The first mark, a dash, is a good starting point because it suggests that there is something to follow. In this case, the rest of the week follows. And although Jesus did not dash into Jerusalem, but rather arrived riding slowly on a donkey, we can remember the day of his entrance into the city, Palm Sunday, by turning the dash into a palm tree. [complete drawing] The quotation marks, which indicate that someone has spoken, need to contain some words, so we will fill in what Jesus named for people in Jerusalem as "the great commandment." [fill in: "Love God."]

Jesus certainly had friends in Jerusalem, but he also had enemies. The bracket, which is used to show how many words or phrases can be drawn together to make one point, reminds us of Jesus' enemies. They drew themselves together against Jesus and wanted to arrest him at the point of a sword. So we will turn the bracket into a sword. [complete drawing] The parentheses are marks that can contain and set apart a particular thought or idea.

On the last night of his life, at a meal we call the Last Supper, Jesus told his friends that every time they met at table and shared a cup together, they should remember him. The time we set apart for Communion uses a cup containing wine/juice; in sharing it, we also remember Jesus. So we will turn the parentheses into a cup. [complete drawing]

On Friday, after a hasty trial, Jesus was sentenced to die. The period is the mark placed at the end of a sentence, so it is fitting to use here. We will turn it into a cross. [complete drawing] After Jesus' death on the cross, his followers were filled with questions. How could this happen? they wondered. Was he truly God's child? What now? Most of all, amidst the questions, they were filled with sadness. So we will turn the question marks into a sorrowful face. [complete drawing] Exclamation marks indicate excitement. They are perfect as reminders of what happened on Easter Day. When the women found Jesus' tomb empty, that was a sign of good news, in fact, the best news ever. We announce that news every Easter with the words I will write in. [write in: Christ is risen, Christ is risen!]

The story of Holy Week did not end. It continues. That is why we have these three dots called an ellipsis at the bottom of the page. This punctuation mark reminds us that followers of Jesus Christ are still on a journey of faith to spread God's love throughout the world. So we will change the ellipsis to footprints into the future. [complete drawing] That is the story of Holy Week, a story from the past, a story to be continued.

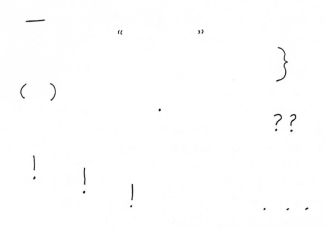

Figure 1

Figure 2

Thanksgiving

Sharing

Materials: Six kernels of corn, bags each containing six kernels of corn—enough bags to provide one for each child present

What do we have here? [show corn and receive responses]

Now what can you do with six kernels of corn, I thought to myself. I came up with several ideas.

You can think of them as your friends—very quiet, dull friends.

You can play games with them by shooting them like marbles or using them as tiny vegetable basketballs by tossing them into a can.

You can plant them, water them, put them in the sunlight; perhaps in a while you will have cornstalks with more corn on them.

You can draw five parallel lines on a piece of paper, paste on the kernels as though they were musical notes, and so make a very brief song.

You can try to stack them—which does not work very well.

You can put them out as a snack for a bird or a squirrel.

You can boil them to make a very small dinner, or you can pop them to have a very short party.

Or . . . you can use them as a reminder to give thanks to God. Why use six kernels of corn that way? Here is the reason: During the first winter that the Pilgrims were in North America, food was so scarce that six kernels of corn a day were all each person was allowed to eat by the time winter was ending. After that terrible season, though, the Pilgrims learned from members of the

Wampanoag tribe how better to plant, grow, and harvest food from the land. And they had food aplenty the next year when they shared in a great Thanksgiving.

I am going to give each one of you a lunch bag containing six kernels of corn, and I would like you and your families to use the bag as a reminder to give God thanks for the food you will be enjoying on Thanksgiving and for all the good gifts of your lives.

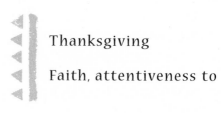

Thanksgiving

Faith, attentiveness to

Materials: Six sheets of paper folded in half and containing the words or phrases described below. The word or phrase shown first and marked with an asterisk is on the left side of the fold, the second is on the right.

1) doz. eggs*
   dog eggs

2) cow*
   sow

3) lots of power*
   loss of power

4) cherry pie*
   cherry pit

5) rug on the floor*
   bug in the flour

6) thanking God*
   thinking God

Changing just one letter in the spelling of a word can turn it into an entirely new word. When that happens, the meaning changes, too, often in a major way. Let me give you some examples.

Sheet #1—Grocery store advertisements regularly invite us to buy a "doz. eggs." Once, however, when I read one of these ads, the "doz. eggs" had been changed by one letter to read [show other half of the sheet] "dog eggs." Maybe if I bought a couple I could hatch out a pair of puppies.

Sheet #2—We know that beef comes from a cow. But a single-letter change turns "cow" into [show the other half of the sheet] "sow." A sow is a pig, and from pigs we get ham. That little letter makes the difference between a hamburger and a ham sandwich.

Sheet #3—Whenever we go for a ride in a kind of motor-driven vehicle, we always hope that the engine has lots of power. But change one letter in that phrase, and it turns into something we hope never happens [show other half of the sheet], a "loss of power." That letter determines whether we arrive where we want to go or have to figure out another way of getting there.

Sheet # 4—Having cherry pie for dessert can be a wonderful treat. But change just one letter and you end up with this [show other half of the sheet]; getting a cherry pit placed on your plate is not such a treat.

Sheet #5—What happens if we change a letter in several words of a phrase? Let's try it. Having a rug on the floor often helps a room feel warmer and cozier. But what about finding a large and lively [show other half of the sheet] bug in the flour when you are baking? Not such a good feeling.

Sheet #6—Over the next week, a week which contains Thanksgiving, I hope we will all be spending some time thanking God for whatever it is we consider our blessings. But how wonderful it would be to try something else as well, something suggested by a single-letter change in the phrase. Try [show other half of the sheet] *thinking* God. Think about how God wants us to use our time; think about how God urges us to treat one another; think about how we can better care for the earth, God's gift to us; think about how we can use our talents to serve and honor God.

You may discover that by thinking God, you do much more thanking God.

Try it!

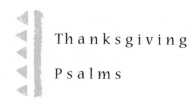

Thanksgiving Psalms

Today we are going to create a psalm of thanksgiving. In order to do that, I would like you to respond to a series of requests. Your responses will be some of the building blocks we use to put together our psalm.

1. Name a kind of song that you like.
2. Name two places anywhere in the world.
3. Name the greatest thing that God does.
4. Name some people that you know.
5. Name some people that you do not know or who are far away.
6. Tell me a word that describes something incredibly powerful.
7. Name something worthless and yucky.
8. Name the most wonderful thing you can think of.
9. Name something bad that can happen to a thing.
10. Tell me how you feel when someone loves you.
11. Name a sound you might make when you are happy or excited.
12. Name something that lives in the ocean.
13. Name something you might find in a field.
14. Name something you could find in the woods.
15. Tell me the best characteristic a person can have.
16. Tell me the best feeling that someone can have.

[Record the children's responses in the corresponding spaces within the text of the psalm. If responses are not forthcoming from the children on particular requests, involve the congregation. A hint: Accept responses as given and use minimal editing.

25

Sometimes those responses that seem most strange are the very ones we most need to hear.]

Many of the psalms in the Old Testament are songs of thanksgiving to God. Today you created a psalm yourselves, not all of it, but part of it. The rest is pretty close to one of the psalms in the Bible (#96). Let's see what we have.

O sing to God a (1) _____ song;
sing to God, (2) _____ and _____ and
    throughout the earth.
Bless God's name
tell of God's (3) _____ from day to day.
Declare God's glory among (4) _____, God's
    marvelous works
among (5) _____.
For (6) _____ is our God, and greatly to be praised.
The gods of the people are as (7) _____,
but our God made (8) _____.
All praise and thanks be to God!

Say among the nations, "God reigns!"
The world shall never (9) _____.
Let the heavens be (10) _____ and let the
    earth (11) _____;
Let the sea roar, and every (12) _____ be glad;
Let the fields exult, and every (13) _____ praise God.
Then shall all the (14) _____ sing for joy in honor
    of our God.
For God comes to judge the world with (15) _____
    and all peoples will (16) _____ .

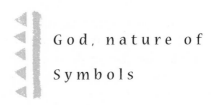

God, nature of

Symbols

One time years ago I went out cross-country skiing and discovered that the snow had much to teach me. That may sound sort of strange to you, so let me explain what I mean, and let me tell you some of what I learned.

1. From the fluffiness of the snow and the way it felt beneath my skis as I glided along, I knew that the temperature had been quite a bit below freezing when the snow fell.

2. As I skied through a grove of trees, I noticed that some of the snow still remained in the branches and that clumps had plopped down here and there right below the trees. There were no drifts anywhere. All these things were the snow's way of letting me know that the wind had been calm since the storm.

3. Footprints in the snow told me the number and approximate size of people who had walked where I was skiing.

4. In one place, the markings in the snow told a story. A mouse trail ended in a patch of disturbed snow. Imprinted there I could see the outline of a hawk's outstretched wings. I knew that the bird had caught its dinner on the run—the snow made that clear.

5. As I looked around, the fluffy shapes that rose from the ground hinted at rocks or stumps or bushes underneath. I could almost imagine what the area would look like without the snow.

6. The snow let me know where I had come from; my ski track followed me all the way and it led me right back to where I had begun.

You may be wondering why I am telling you all this here in church. Well, it occurred to me that the way God teaches us is much like the way snow teaches us—quietly, honestly, clearly, often through symbols or signs. And we should take note that in order to learn we have to be very observant of our surroundings and of ourselves. We have to be alert, and we have to learn *how* to learn what the snow, or God, has to teach us. Together, that is what we try to do in our worship, our classes, our programs and activities.

Faith

Keys

Materials: A key case with house and church keys, a set of car keys, a post office box key, an unidentified key (old, if possible)

During the past week, I have been very much aware of keys. The people I work with often asked to borrow mine; I kept trying to remember which pocket or drawer I had left them in; one key that had always worked fine suddenly started sticking; a friend lost all his keys.

Keys are rather important items because they open things up, get machines to work, and help us stay alert as we try to keep track of them. They are also reminders about our faith. I have brought along some of the keys I carry to show you what I mean by that.

1. These are the keys to my house and to the church [show]. [*Note:* If a layperson is presenting this message, children will gain the additional understanding that not just clergy have keys to the church building!] They tell me every day that it is important to have a home for faith, a place where we can be accepted and loved, where we can share our concerns and abilities, where we are always welcome. The church is such a place. And if we put our faith to it, where we live and where we work and where we go to school can be such places as well.

2. These are keys to a car [show]. They inform me that faith is meant to be something that moves—that moves us to feel, moves us to do for others, moves us closer to God. All of these things will require us to keep our faith fueled up and well maintained.

3. These are keys to a post office box [show]. They remind me that as we grow in faith there will always be surprises. Whenever I open the post office box, I am entirely ready and eager to be surprised by finding something other than bills or junk mail— maybe a favorite magazine or a real letter from a friend. Faith also has many surprises for us when we open it up.

4. This is a key to what [show]? Actually, I was hoping you might know since I have been wondering about it for a long time! This key is a reminder to me that there will always be things a bit mysterious about faith, things we cannot seem to open up and understand. But we need to keep a key ready—maybe some day it will be just what we need.

5. [Hold up "invisible key."] This is the key that opens us up to one another. It is a key of faith, and we offer it to God, to family or friends (people we trust), so they can enter our lives to encourage us, guide us, be with us in caring and love.

I hope that talking about keys has opened up a few new ways of looking at our faith. Now I will put them all away—definitely somewhere I will be able to find them!

Love

Parables

The following tale is a wintertime story about love.

There was once a boy named Sherman. He was eight years old. On a cold and lonely winter day in the hungry late afternoon before supper, Sherman found himself thinking about what love meant. Actually, he was feeling a bit unlovable and unloving, and somehow sensed that he needed to find out what he was missing. He said to himself: "Nobody's ever told me what love is. I'm going to ask my neighbors and friends." So he threw on his coat and ran out the door.

His first stop was old Mrs. Scheller down the block. "Can you tell me what love is?" he asked. "No, not really," she replied. Then she noticed that he was blowing on his hands. "Your hands must be freezing, Sherman. I just finished knitting some mittens. I think one of the pairs will fit you." She fetched a pair and they did fit, even with a little growing room. Sherman thanked her as he left though he was disappointed she had not answered his question.

Mr. Green lived two houses away from Mrs. Scheller. "Can you tell me what love is?" Sherman asked as soon as he stepped inside. "Not sure I can," came the response. Sherman sighed. Mr. Green, who was a commercial artist, said, "You really like watching me work, don't you, Sherman?" The boy nodded enthusiastically. "Then let me show you something. By the way, what's your favorite animal?" Sherman named the raccoon. Over the next quarter hour, Mr. Green showed Sherman how to draw a raccoon, and when he left, Sherman was holding a pretty good picture of a plump raccoon that he had drawn himself. But he still had not gotten an answer to his question.

His next stop was at the home of the Tilsons, whose two children were off at school. "Can you tell me what love is?" Sherman inquired. Mrs. Tilson said, "I don't exactly think we can tell you. Maybe we can just sit down and share a small piece of pie together—small enough so it won't spoil your dinner. Vaughan and I made an apple pie this afternoon. You do look hungry, Sherman." Sherman admitted he was *very* hungry. So they shared pie and had a great visit. Still, he did not get his question answered.

Finally, Sherman stopped by the house of his friend Jerome. "I've asked all the grown-ups I can think of what love is. They don't have a clue. Can you tell me, Jerome?" But all Jerome said was: "You know, I missed having you come over when you were sick earlier this week. Let's play something." So they did.

While Sherman was out, his mother had received phone calls from Mrs. Scheller, Mr. Green, the Tilsons, and Jerome's mother. All of them wanted her to know where Sherman was, and they each gave a brief account of the visits.

When Sherman arrived back home, he flopped on the sofa and said: "I've asked everyone else. I might as well ask you. Can you tell me what love is?" She said, "Maybe I can. Let me tell you a story." And she told him a story about a child much like him who went off to ask his neighbors the exact same question. One of his neighbors gave mittens to the child in the story so his hands would not get cold; another taught the child a new and exciting skill; another kept the child from starving; another offered glad and eager friendship. His mother ended the story by saying, "I think that through all those things the neighbors did, the child really did get an answer to the question."

Sherman looked at his mother. She was smiling a funny little smile that told him she was not going to answer any further questions. Somehow that was all right.

When people asked questions of Jesus about love and about God and about themselves, he often answered them with actions (as the neighbors did), and he often answered them with stories called parables (as Sherman's mother did). One of the most important things we can ever learn about our faith is that it asks us to show/express the love of God in all our actions, in every day of our life story.

Grace

Thankfulness

Last week I went bowling. The object of the game, as many of you know, is to roll a heavy ball toward ten pins so as to knock them all down. When you do this, it is called a strike. But to get a strike, you have to roll the ball *just right*. During one game last week, I rolled the ball all wrong. An amazing thing happened, though. The pins fell slowly and weirdly sideways and forward. *All* of them fell down—it was a strike. I filled in my score sheet and said to myself, "I really didn't deserve that."

That strange strike got me thinking about other times I had felt as though I had not deserved what I received. A few things came to mind.

Once, while I was fishing at a small pond on an evening with no bugs and a warm breeze, I looked up, and there standing against a sky colored sunset-rose were five deer nibbling on their supper of leaves. And as if that were not enough, just at that moment a large bass took my lure and I had my own supper on the line. I did nothing to deserve that beautiful sight and that excitement, but I was thankful for it.

I also thought back to a tradition in my family of "liking-gifts." These were little presents we sometimes gave to another member of the family for no special occasion at all, not a birthday or an anniversary or any other holiday. No one earned or deserved "liking-gifts"; they came as surprises just to say, "I like you," and the only way to respond when you got one was with, "Thank you."

Positively the biggest gift I ever received that I did nothing to deserve was the gift of life itself. It is a magnificent, holy gift to be treasured every day. Here, thank God, *I am;* and here, thank God, *you are,* too.

Throughout our lives, we receive gifts that come to us not because we deserve them, but because someone, or God, loves us so much that the love absolutely has to be expressed and given. When this kind of giving goes on, it is called "grace." Our faith tells us that God is amazingly, wonderfully gracious; our faith encourages us to be gracious, as well, toward all people. I hope you will think about the ways God's grace is real to you and about how you might enjoy creating ways to let others feel that grace.

I think you will discover that a graceful/grace-filled life is also a thankful/thanks-filled one.

[*Note:* This resource may be adapted in many ways to make it personal to the presenter.]

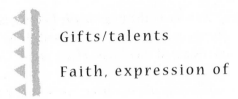

Resource: A skilled guitarist

This morning, my friend Mr./Ms. _____ and his/her friend are going to help with our children's time. Mr./Ms. _____ is a person. What is the friend? (a guitar)

In order to get sounds and music from a guitar, what do you do with it? (strum, pluck the strings) Mr./Ms. _____ will give an example of strumming and plucking the strings. There we have it. Those are the sounds that a guitar makes. Right?

Actually, there are many other kinds of sounds that can come from a guitar. I am going to have Mr./Ms. _____ and his/her friend show what those sounds are.

[The options are many. I have listed several possibilities.]

1. hammer on note
2. pull off note
3. tap body of guitar
4. play harmonics
5. bend note
6. demonstrate bottleneck style
7. play harp tones
8. demonstrate two-handed fretboard tapping

The guitar looks very simple to play, and we expect certain sounds from it. But when Mr./Ms. _____ and his/her friend work together, some amazing and wonderful things happen. The guitar can do what we might never imagine it could do.

Sometimes when we look at other people, or at ourselves, we do not imagine enough. We think there is not much we can do or not much we can be. And that may be true if we only pluck or strum at our lives, if we try to get by on our own. *But,* if we use all the imagination we have and if we really put ourselves in God's hands, amazing and wonderful things can happen. We will not necessarily discover new sounds, but we will discover new ideas, new talents, new goals, new hopes, new ways of helping and serving others.

Mr./Ms. _____ and his/her friend can make beautiful and exciting music together; when we think of our lives as a friendship and partnership with God, we can find beauty and excitement in every day.

God's love

Choices

Materials: Music book, storybook, peanut butter sandwich, sandwich made with shredded newspaper, water balloon, air balloon

What things are filled with makes a difference in how we can use them.

If you want to read [hold up music book and storybook], the filling makes a difference in determining whether you will sing the words or listen to them as a story.

If you are hungry [hold up peanut butter sandwich and sandwich made with shredded newspaper], the filling makes a difference in determining whether you will be nourished and satisfied or not.

If you feel like playing a game [hold up water balloon and air balloon], the filling certainly makes a difference in determining what kind of game you will play.

What people are filled with makes a difference, too.

We can be filled with hatred; we can be filled with love.
We can be filled with sneakiness; we can be filled
with honesty.
We can be filled with anger; we can be filled with hope.
We can be filled with so many thoughts, feelings,
attitudes, beliefs.

What we are filled with makes a difference in what *we* can be used for, what we can do, how we look at the world around us, how we treat others.

One of the things we do in the church is to try to learn together how we can choose well what to be filled with. Some good choices, some tried-and-true choices for all of us are these: God's love and Spirit and caring. Let them fill you, and see what happens!

Healing

Materials: A jar of honey, an aloe plant, a picture of sunshine

I am going to give you a few lists of things right now, and I would like you to tell me what they have in common, that is, how they are in some way the same. Ready?

One, three, five, seven, nine (all odd numbers)

Dog, rabbit, giraffe, aardvark, turtle (all animals)

The Atlantic Ocean, the [name of nearby or familiar river], the air outside in a rainstorm, the drinking glass underneath the pulpit [use "on a speaker's table" if no pulpit is present] (all have water in them)

Trains, boats, planes, trucks (all take people or cargo from one place to another)

Now for a harder list. What do these things have in common?

Honey, an aloe plant, kisses and kind words, sunshine, God

The answer? All of these can help heal people.

[Show honey] Honey has long been used as a natural antiseptic to help heal cuts and insect bites.

[Show aloe] Aloe is especially useful in soothing burns.

[Kisses and kind words] There are all sorts of hurts and pains that get treated effectively with kisses or kind words.

[Show picture of sunshine] Many people feel that sunshine helps us get better when we have a cold.

And what about God? The Bible tells us that God worked through Jesus Christ and through the power of the Spirit to heal people of all kinds of hurts. Illnesses. Fears. Injustices. And God calls us to be healers, too, to bring others to health and to treat them as whole persons. We can be part of God's ministry of healing by praying, by caring, by trying to "help the hurt go away" whatever kind it is.

Faith, creativity of

Gifts/talents

Materials: A tennis racquet, the picture provided (or a replica), spaghetti

If I didn't know what this object was [show racquet], I might think of all sorts of things it could be used for.

It could be used to help me draw designs. I made this one [show design] by following some of the strings with a pen so I got little boxes; then I colored in a few of the boxes.

This could be used for measuring servings of spaghetti [show how spaghetti fits through squares formed by the strings]. I found out that four of the top squares were just the right amount for one person's portion.

This could certainly be used for beating a dusty rug or a floor mat; it is great for smacking the dirt out.

This could be used as a sort of flyswatter-with-a-heart. It gives the fly a sporting chance to get away through one of the squares.

This could be used at parties to serve fancy little sandwiches or desserts. It has a nice long handle and a non-slip grip.

It could be used for lots of other things—to put over your face when you lie outside so you get a fancy suntan; to use as a canoe paddle if you don't want to go very fast . . . we could probably come up with lots of other uses.

Most of you, though, know what its best use is. What is that? [responses]

How are we a bit like this tennis racquet? Well, think about this: One of the things we try to learn with one another in the church is what our best use is as people. That means trying to figure out how we can do our best to love God, to help others, to discover all our talents. When we do all those things, we are not only put to good use as human beings, we are also put to God's use. It may take a while to figure out our best use; when we do, it may surprise us. But it will probably also "feel right" and provide us with tremendous enjoyment.

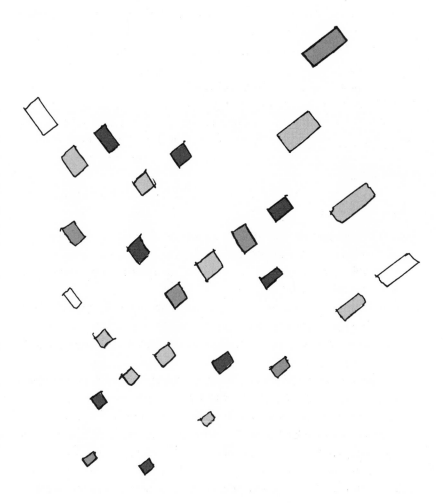

Unity

Fellowship

Do any of you know what the word "united" means? [responses]

There are many ways of expressing the meaning of "united," but basically, it means bringing a number of things together into one whole.

One way I enjoy uniting things is mixing different kinds of fruit together into one big fruit salad.

When I was looking at the pieces of fruit in a salad the other day, their variety suddenly made me think of the variety of people at church. I imagined the church as something like a giant fruit salad.

Let me tell you what I mean. There are people who are a great deal like each kind of fruit.

- Some people are apples . . . sort of shiny and crisp, and maybe even a bit saucy
- Some are oranges . . . in need of a squeeze (with people we call that an embrace or hug)
- Some are pineapples . . . prickly and sharp on the outside but sweet on the inside
- Some people are bananas . . . they look tough but bruise easily
- Some are papayas . . . bringing the delicious flavor of another culture or part of the world
- Other folks are peaches . . . fine-and-dandy-and-everything's-peachy types
- And then there are grapes . . . who hang around in bunches
- And lemons . . . who seem sour but who make the whole salad taste better

Just as a fruit salad unites edibles of many different colors and flavors and textures, so a church unites all different kinds of people. It is God's gift to us that we can unite for worship and fellowship and service. We are meant to be together—a big fruit salad of people.

[*Note:* This piece can be embellished and expanded in a number of ways. The options are especially wide for persons in churches having the word "united" in their denominational names (United Church of Christ and United Methodist Church, for example).]

Forgiveness

I remember the first time I ever felt what it was to be forgiven. While I tell you about that, I want all of you in the congregation to think of some time when *you* were forgiven, to try to remember what it meant to you. I am hoping that some of you will share an example and a feeling.

Many times as a child I had done things wrong, said I was sorry, and been forgiven, but one day when I was about twelve a neighbor helped me really start to understand forgiveness. While I was mowing her lawn, rushing so I could get to a baseball game, I ran over her favorite plant. It was a very unusual, valuable plant that I had been told to be particularly careful of. The woman loved that plant. It is actually not correct to say I ran over it—in fact, I shredded it. What I remember is looking down and seeing little bits of color in the grass, bright blues that used to be the plant. I felt heavy in my heart. I walked over to my neighbor's door, waited, did not look up when she opened it, and said: "I'm sorry. I ran over your plant and you can't even see it any more 'cept for some bluish grass." I expected her to yell or cry. Instead she said, "You must feel terrible. I forgive you." Then she told me to finish up the lawn. When I left that day, my neighbor handed me a couple of cookies with the words, "I hope these will make you feel better." Being forgiven made the heaviness go away, let me be thankful, and helped me decide (as I wiped cookie crumbs from my mouth) that I would always do an especially good job on that neighbor's lawn.

Would anyone in the congregation like to share an experience that helped bring about an understanding of forgiveness and the feeling it brings?

[Examples by congregants]

Forgiveness is one of God's greatest gifts to the world. Learn about it; accept it; feel it.

One of Jesus' best-known stories/parables is about forgiveness. The story tells of a child who is foolish and bratty, a parent who is loving, and a brother who is the kind of guy who would have screamed at me if I had mowed down his plant. We call this story the parable of the prodigal son. Read it!

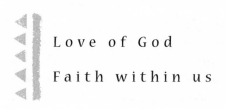

Love of God

Faith within us

Over the past few weeks, I have noticed something while driving around: People carry all sorts of stuff with them inside their cars. That shelf behind the backseat provides a spot for toys, bobbing-head dolls, sun-bleached books, and, in one case, a small planter with a cactus in it. Rearview mirrors get decorated with fuzzy dice, crystals and feathers, graduation tassels. On windows, people put funny (or not so funny) signs, pigs or Garfields with suction-cup feet, and a variety of college or organization decals. All these items tell something about the people in the car—about what they think is cute or funny or important, about connections with certain schools or groups.

Lots of other items help us form a picture of the folks associated with cars. A backseat full of suitcases and a rack of clothes often means that someone is on a vacation or a business trip. A child seat is a pretty fair indication of a resident youngster under five years of age. By counting the number of grocery bags tucked inside a vehicle, you can make an educated guess at family size. The wrappings or remainders of food in a car are a clue to someone's eating habits. A good number of things people take with them are items that tell the kind of work they do—samples of products they sell, tools of their trade, special equipment, books or magazines about their job or profession. And most of us have in our cars some clues about the things we like to do for enjoyment. For example, inside my car I have (tennis balls, running shoes, fishing tackle, roller blades, etc.).

What we carry around inside our cars does tell about us. But what we carry around inside ourselves tells even more. Hatred, anger, grudges, caring, kindness, hope—these are just some of the possibilities. And whatever is there, others will see it through our actions as clearly as through glass car windows. Here in the church, we try to encourage you to carry inside yourselves the love of God, to have it with you always—never to be without it and ever willing to let others see that love whenever they are near you. To have such a love within you and to use it says more about you than anything else.

Communion

Grace

Seeing the Communion table set and ready always reminds me of my family's table back when I was growing up. It is even about the same size, though the one at home was a bit shorter and a touch wider.

Whenever we gathered at that table, my job was to say the prayer before the meal, the one we call grace. While Mom, Dad, and my sister listened, I would say, "Thank you for this food and for all the blessings of the day. In Jesus' name, Amen." Most of the time the food was to my liking and I could usually think of something that happened during the day that I might call a blessing. Often, both the food and the day were very good, so thanks came easily and quickly. When I was especially hungry and excited, the grace came out as: "Thnkyufrthsfudnfrallablssngsvthday. InJzznmamn." And my hand would be on the fork faster than anyone could open their eyes.

One day I had had a crummy time at school and a mopey afternoon with no one to play with, but I was hungry and looking forward to supper. When I sat down at the table I could not believe what I saw. Two serving dishes, one filled with corned beef hash and the other with asparagus. What had I done to deserve this? For I hated them both. I got up to look in the refrigerator for some saving dessert. Lime gelatin with pineapple. Yuck.

Upon returning to the table, I sat in a sort of daze, and Mom had to tap my arm and say, "It's time to say grace." And for the first time ever, I said, "Do I have to?" Mom replied, "Of course." So I mumbled a very unthankful thank-you to God for food I did not like and blessings I did not see. Then I opened my eyes, and I saw Dad with a big smile going for the hash he loved, and I watched Mom carefully pick out tender asparagus stalks that were a special treat to her, and I remembered how much my sister liked lime gelatin. All of a sudden, I was glad to have said grace. And I understood that the thanks for the meal was for more than food or anything that had happened in the day. It was for the sharing of being at the table. So I poured lots of ketchup on the hash, pretended the slippery asparagus was something tastier (like worms), and spooned down shivers of gelatin with a smile.

The gathering for Communion at table here is rather like that supper I described in a couple of ways: it is a family supper of love and sharing, and it is a time for being glad we can offer thanks to God. These are things to remember whenever we come to the table.

[*Note:* This story may be adapted in many ways to make it personal to the presenter.]

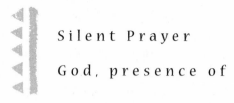

Silent Prayer

God, presence of

Materials: A wristwatch

[Show wristwatch] Can any of you tell me what this is?

It's a watch. And because it is worn on a wrist, we often call it a wristwatch.

Now if I were to say the words "whale watch," would you think immediately of a huge clock face with numbers as big as I am and a strap made out of chains? Would you think of something a whale would put around itself so it could tell time? Or would you think of something else?

I hope you would think of something else, because when most people (except for the very strangest) mention a whale watch, they are talking about a boat trip taken by passengers who want to look for and watch whales. Some time back, I went on a whale watch one foggy day. The captain of the boat I was on told the passengers, when we were out in the ocean a ways, that he was sure a whale was nearby. You see, the fish finder he had on board showed a bunch of fish deep below—just what a whale would feed upon. So we watched carefully. The fog made that hard to do, but soon we saw the backs of a couple of minke whales and later on we saw the back of a big finback whale. The captain told us that what we saw—which looked plenty large to us—was only about a fifth of the whale's length. Most of the huge animal remained hidden under water. We also sat for a while in the boat as it drifted with its engines off. Everyone aboard kept quiet, and every now and then we would hear a "whoooosh" as a whale

46

came to the surface to exhale and to get a new supply of air. We could not see the animal through the fog, yet we could hear it and feel it nearby.

Being on that whale watch reminded me of the way people of faith look for God in their lives. Just as that captain knew a whale was around when he saw fish down deep, we can know that God will be wherever needs and hopes are deep within us. Just as there was much more to the whale than we could see, there is always much more to God than we can ever understand. And just as our quietness allowed us to hear and feel a whale's presence, often we can best become aware of God when we are most quiet in thought or in prayer.

 Jesus Christ, putting on

Materials: heavy winter gloves, yard work gloves, baseball glove, latex rubber gloves, archery glove. [Other kinds of gloves, ones specifically suited to the speaker, may be used.]

I was thinking this past week that what we put on tells a great deal about what we plan to do. See if you can tell what I might be about to do just by looking at what I put on my hands.

1. Heavy winter gloves—[responses] These suggest that I plan to be going outside for snow shoveling, hiking, skiing, or playing. They are not for typing at my desk or for eating.

2. Yard work gloves—[responses] These suggest that I will be working in a yard or garden, or perhaps I will be lifting things and so need protection for my hands. They are not for making bread or playing the guitar.

3. Baseball glove—[responses] This is useful, even necessary, for playing baseball. It is not what I would wear when preaching a sermon.

4. Latex rubber gloves—[responses] These indicate that I might be about to do surgery or dental work, or I might be using chemicals or dangerous materials. They are not what I would wear to a party.

5. Archery glove—[responses] These I put on before shooting a bow and arrow. They are not for making snowballs or for pulling weeds in the garden.

What I put on my hands affects what I can do or will do with them.

One of the most important writers in the Bible, the apostle Paul, told his friends that to show their faith they should "put on Christ." What he meant by that, I believe, is that he wanted them to imagine, to act, to deal with other folks just as Jesus Christ would. "Before you do anything," he said, "put on Christ." That is something quite amazing to think about. If you put on Christ—if you really had Christ as part of you—how would you use your time? How would you treat other people? What would you do differently from what you do now? What would be most important to you? I do not want you to answer these questions right now, but I hope you will think about them and talk about them with your friends and family.

Commonplace/Miracles

used 6/25/06

[*Note:* The following story is offered as an example of how rec-
ollections of childhood might serve as parables, as a means of
sharing faith in a simple and forthright manner.]

During my years of childhood, I had a friend named Eddie. Eddie
was an active boy, but not a rough-and-tumble type like some of
my other friends. Let me put it this way: Eddie was my favorite
indoors and rainy-day friend. He was the kind of person who
would not drive my parents crazy if we stayed inside to play. I
want to tell you about one day when it rained.

We played all day racing cars, shooting darts, trading baseball
cards, reading comics, fooling around. We got special permission
to eat in the living room where we could watch cartoons. I remember Bugs Bunny and I remember not spilling anything.

Eddie was a teacher to me, but I did not know it at the time.
He taught me to look at things closely—like how racing cars held
the track as they sped through turns. He taught me to look for
things—like how the darts formed patterns on the board. That
rainy day we watched what the wind did to the rain droplets
caught in the fine screen of the living room windows. Usually, the
wind blew the droplets into designs, but sometimes into whole
pictures. Eddie spotted most of them first.

That day he told me something I will never forget. As we
knelt watching the rain patterns, a draft of wind from around the
window blew a small ball of dust onto the windowsill in front of
us. Eddie reached gently for the dust, licking his fingers first so it
would stick to them. He held it between his thumb and forefin-
ger away from our faces so the light from a lamp across the room

49

shined through it. There were light colors in it, soft, surprising colors. Eddie's eyes grew wide. He turned to me, almost breathless. "Look! See! Even this is a miracle."

He was right. Eddie showed me that even in common, ordinary things there was always something miraculous and new. I appreciated learning this in my childhood, and I wanted to share it with you. Whenever you look at yourselves, at one another, at the world around you, remember the way Eddie saw things, and so be alert for whatever is miraculous and new.

God, presence of

Materials: A battery-operated CD/tape player, a mechanical windup toy, a wristwatch, an electric pencil sharpener (and access to an outlet)

I am going to show you four objects that I enjoy using.

The first one is this [show CD/tape player]. Sometimes I like listening to music while I am working or reading, so I pop in a CD or a cassette. My favorite tunes are right at my fingertips. I do not know exactly what is inside this box, but when I press the start button [press it], I have *confidence* that music will fill the air.

The second object is this little mechanical figure. (Grown-ups are allowed to have toys, too!) I do not know what is inside it, but I *believe* completely that whenever I turn this stem and set it down, it will take off walking [or provide a description of whatever it is the toy does]. Somehow, watching this thing always makes me feel a bit happier.

The third object is actually something I wear. It is this watch. I do not look at it very often, though when I am planning to meet someone or getting ready for a meeting, I certainly do then. I also look at the stopwatch portion of it when I go out for a walk or a jog. I do not know what is inside this to make the numbers appear and change, but I *trust* it to show me exactly what time it is or how much time has gone by.

The final thing I want to show you is this nifty pencil sharpener. I use pencils a lot for sketching, for jotting down notes, for writing in my appointment book. So I wear them down quickly. I do not know what is inside this machine—maybe a crew of tiny people with chain saws—but I have *faith* that when I put in a dull pencil [do so], a sharp one will come out.

Though we cannot see inside any of these objects, whatever is inside them powers them into action. That something inside is also what allows me to have confidence, to believe, to trust, and to have faith that the objects will do what they are supposed to do. This is rather similar to the way it is with us. We have probably learned that inside us we have quarts of blood and bunches of organs, numerous bones and layers of muscles. Science books tell us this. But the Bible tells us something else, something extraordinary. The apostle Paul writes that "God is at work *in you*." That is an amazing thing to think about. God is in us to give us the power—the Spirit—to act, to do what is best, what is loving and caring and just and true. No one can see God inside, but when we act in those ways, we can begin to feel God at work in ourselves. And we can understand better how God works in and through others.

Our faith consistently reminds us that God is with us; it also gives us the good news that God is within us.

Creation/Creativity

A girl named Suki decided that she wanted a pet—a rabbit, to be exact. So being a clever person, she decided to make one. It seemed like a good idea. First she made a rabbit out of clay. It was a great rabbit with long stiff ears, threads for whiskers, buttons for eyes, and a small doorknob for a tail. The problem was, however, that even though it looked like a rabbit, it did not hop, was not cuddly, and had no interest in eating carrots. Back to some more planning.

Suki began a second rabbit. This one she made out of cotton, and she used two big springs for the hind legs so it could jump. Well, this rabbit certainly was cuddly (except for its springs). It could hop a few feet with each jump, but it left a weird trail on the ground and still had no interest in eating carrots. Suki was getting quite frustrated, so she asked another clever friend to help. Jorge quickly took out a carving knife and cut a piece of wood so it looked quite a bit like a rabbit. But—you guessed it— it did not hop, was not cuddly, and had no interest in eating carrots. It also gave splinters when you tried to pet it. A sad situation it was.

Finally, the two friends put their clever brains together on one more rabbit. They formed its body out of wood, made a hollow head from papier-mâché, covered it all with cotton, and attached felt feet to legs made from springs. And best of all, they put a pencil sharpener inside their rabbit so that when you stuck a carrot stick into its mouth and cranked its ear, it would eat the carrot. The two friends thought this creation was a wonderful pet for Suki. Their rabbit hopped, felt cuddly, looked like a rabbit, and even seemed to eat carrots. But something, they discovered, was missing. What was that? [responses] Yes, the rabbit they made was the best they could do, but it was not alive. It was a real fake rabbit but not a real real rabbit. (By the way, Suki later got a real rabbit from a friend who lived on a farm.)

The world around us is alive with wonders, and we believe that God began this whole world and cares for it always. Even if we are very clever, we cannot make a rabbit or a tree or an earth-surrounding atmosphere. But God caused all these things, and more, to be made, and we are indeed thankful.

What those two friends learned or remembered was something all of us should never forget. There is good reason why we call God the Creator with a capital "C," for God alone gives life. If we are thoughtful and sensitive (and creative with our living faith), we will give thanks to God often for that gift of life. Remember:

No matter how you carve it, shape it, assemble it or prefab it,
Only God can make a rabbit.

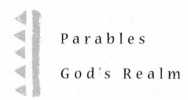

Parables

God's Realm

Jesus' favorite way of teaching people was sharing with them little stories called parables. Often, the parable would tell what it is like to live in a place God rules, a place we call God's realm. Today you are going to help create a parable. I have part of one in front of me, but it is not complete; there are blank spaces to fill in. If you can name the things I ask you to name, I think we can fill in the blanks and so finish the parable. Let's try.

1. Name a kind of person you are afraid of _____
2. Name a person or group of persons you like _____
3. Name a disease _____
4. Name something bad that people do _____
5. Name something beautiful _____
6. Name something you care about a lot _____
7. Name something that grows _____
8. Name a happy time or event _____

Thank you!

If Jesus came to talk with us, he would probably tell us a parable. It might sound something like this:

God's realm is alive with surprise and topsy-turvy.

In it you find that *(1)* _____ can be your friend, and you will love being with him or her as much as being with *(2)* _____ .

The light in God's realm will heal all who live there. People with *(3)* _____ will be made whole. People who *(4)* _____ will *(4)* _____ no more.

The environment of God's realm will have the beauty of *(5)* _____ for people will care about it as much as for *(6)* _____ .

You will grow in God's realm as fast/big/strong/wondrously as a *(7)* _____ . And every moment will be like a *(8)* _____ as you worship God.

After telling the parable, Jesus would probably ask, "Do you want to live there?" And if you said, "Yes!" he would say, "Follow me!"

Church (especially a "Church Awareness Day")

Materials: A rubber ball, a small calculator, a book

There is a song in a musical (*The Sound of Music*) that speaks of "raindrops on roses and whiskers on kittens, bright copper kettles and warm woolen mittens, brown paper packages tied up with strings." The singer says that these are a few of her favorite things.

They are not my favorite things. But this morning I brought with me a few items that are. And one of the reasons they are favorites is that something invisible is going on within them or happening to them beyond what can be seen.

1. [Show ball] This ball, or almost any ball, is one of my favorite things. You can *see* what it does [bounce ball], but the

gravity that pulls it down and the springiness that lets it bounce back are both invisible.

2. [Show calculator] This little instrument does calculations as fast as I can press the keys. Answers get pictured on the small screen so I can use the results for whatever purpose I need. But the real work of the calculator is done by tiny chips inside and by electrons racing through circuits—things totally invisible to me.

3. [Show book] Books are favorite things. What you see are words on pages, but beyond them are all sorts of invisible characters and settings that can be seen only with the imagination. And there is also an invisible writer somewhere who put the words together.

4. Living is one of my favorite things, so I brought along [point] myself. It is pretty obvious that I am alive, but all sorts of invisible things are keeping me that way—lungs and heart and brain and God's love.

5. Finally, one of my favorite things, and I hope yours, is the church. Just as with all these other things, the church has objects and activities and programs everyone can see. However, it also has some highly important parts that are invisible unless you take a good look. Behind-the-scenes work. Forms of outreach that help people in our own community and around the world. Keeping the church property in good condition and planning ahead. Visits and kindnesses. Prayerfulness and quiet giving. Today some members of the congregation will be telling you about a number of the "invisibles" that go on within this favorite thing we call the church.

[Note: This resource is designed for a "Church Awareness Day." Church officers and representatives of boards/committees/groups can explain to children the "invisibles."]

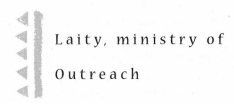

Laity, ministry of
Outreach

A couple of questions . . .

How many of you would like to be ministers when you grow up? [responses]

[*Note:* If there is an active visitation ministry by deacons, the language of this resource piece may be adapted to fit such a situation.]

How many ministers are there in this building now? [responses]

There are as many ministers as there are people in the building. The word "minister" ("deacon") is actually just another name for servant, a person who helps meet the needs of others. One of the things we believe as followers of Jesus Christ is that every single person can serve others by loving them and caring about them. The fancy name for this is "the priesthood of all believers." What that means in general is that God always has something for us to do, some ways we can be thoughtful and helpful and caring and loving toward other folks. What that means to me is that I have plenty of assistant ministers. The people sitting in the pews (seats) today—parents, neighbors, friends—are ministers. The place is loaded with ministers, people who serve! They do all kinds of jobs in the church, and we hope that God's love comes to life through what they do.

One thing I often do in my particular ministry is visit people who are in hospitals or ill at home or unable to get out for one reason or another. Often, these people are a bit sad or lonely or uncomfortable. Almost always, they are very glad to see me and to hear me say that their church family loves them. What I would like to ask *you* to do is to come with me on some of these visits, not in

57

person, because many of the visits are during school hours (now you really would like to come along!), but by making a picture that I can give to the person I visit. By putting your heart and mind and imagination into the picture, you can come along with me. Think of it as creating a "get-well-we-miss-you-and-love-you" card, and put on it a drawing or painting of something that you believe could cheer someone who is feeling blue. Bring the pictures back to me next Sunday or before, and during the next few weeks I will pass them out. Those who receive them will be very thankful. And I will be thankful, too, for your help as assistant ministers.

Giving

Stewardship

Materials: Envelope containing letter, envelope containing magazine, envelope containing bill, envelope containing sweepstakes forms, envelopes containing powdered cocoa and dry soup, envelope containing seeds, church/church school envelopes

I brought a whole handful of things with me this morning. [hold up all the envelopes] What are all of these? [responses] Let's take a look at the envelopes and what is inside them.

1. [Show letter] This envelope contains a letter from a friend. A letter is usually something that is fun to get.

2. [Show magazine] When we open this envelope, we find a magazine. Magazines are often fun to get.

3. [Show bill] This envelope has a bill inside. I receive lots of these; they are not fun to get.

4. [Show sweepstakes forms] The contents of this envelope tell me that I have an opportunity to win two million dollars and will therefore never have to worry about bills again. The small catch is that I have to buy something in order to enter—for which I will receive a bill.

5. [Show cocoa and soup envelopes] Both these envelopes contain food, the kind of food that looks rather unappetizing in its present form but smells and tastes wonderful after hot water is added.

6. [Show seed envelopes] The seeds in this envelope will produce (name of chosen plant) if we plant them and care for them.

If all these envelopes had nothing in them when we opened them up, they would not seem very useful, would they?

What kind of envelopes are these? [hold up church/church school offering envelopes] In order for these to be useful, they need to have something put in them. We ask that people put in offerings of money as thank-you's to God, as support for doing God's work throughout the world, as help in paying for all the activities of this church. Whatever we receive in these envelopes gets well used in doing the ministry we all share.

[*Note:* This lesson can readily lead into an explanation/discussion of how funds are used in the church. If there is a special church school project (for example, child sponsorship, Heifer Project, Habitat for Humanity, missionary support, etc.) funded by children's offerings, this may be introduced or explained.]

Church Symbols

Materials: The five pictures provided

Today is the day of our church's annual meeting, and that got me thinking about sharing some pictures with you, pictures of things that are symbols for the church. Most of these have been used for many years, but the final one I thought up last week. Here they are.

1. [Show picture of house] The church is sometimes called the house of God. That fits, for it is here where we are aware of God's presence, here where we often find ourselves "at home" with God. The symbol makes it clear why congregations are referred to as faith families.

2. [Show picture of beehive] This is an extremely old symbol. In a beehive, all the individual bees work for the common good of the hive; in a church, common mission makes use of individual skills and talents. Also, a church tends to be like a beehive because so many activities are going on.

3. [Show picture depicting Jesus] Through the centuries, the church has been called the body of Christ. This, too, is a good name and a good symbol, for the church is the body of people who try to show how Christ is alive and at work in the world.

4. [Show picture of ship upon the water] The ship is also an ancient symbol. The rough water illustrates the storms that churches must face on their journey of faith; the cross-shaped mast serves as reminder of the presence of Christ that will carry the church through.

5. [Show picture of stew pot and spoon] Now for the new symbol. I thought that a pot of beef stew and a spoon were ex-

cellent images for the church. Let me explain: God is the good stock and the spices that give the church its flavor. Jesus' teachings are the meat and vegetables that nourish us and give us strength. The Spirit is the wonderful, inviting smell that draws us in. We are the bowl and the spoon that hold God's love/presence inside us, that offer it to others, that keep things stirred up in this world.

Which symbol do you like best? Think about it—and perhaps you can come up with symbols of your own.

Church

Puzzle

Materials: Puzzle pieces (as described and shown), adhesive tape

Christ's church is a somewhat puzzling body. It has many different forms, but it is also one whole. Its basic task is making the invisible love of God visible in the world. It welcomes into a single family people from all places and races, all ages of life and stages of faith.

If we were to think of the church as a gigantic jigsaw puzzle, each one of us would be a piece of that puzzle. To get a full picture of the church, we have to fit together our individual gifts and talents. Today, as we begin our church school year (Or: as we begin a new quarter/semester, as we begin our vacation church school, etc.), every one of you will receive a puzzle piece. It may not seem important. It may not even have anything drawn or written upon it. Yet we cannot get the whole picture without having every piece used. After the class portions of the puzzle are complete, one of the teachers will collect them and put them together to create a picture we will display. When you look at that picture, let it remind you how we need one another in order truly to be the church.

[The puzzle, drawn or painted on poster board, should be divided into a number of rectangles corresponding to the number of classes. Each rectangle gets cut up so as to provide one piece per student. Use the maximum number for each class; if there are extra pieces, these can be used to show that we need to remember persons who are absent or who might join the class. Once fitted, the pieces can be held together by using tape on the reverse side. Assembling the rectangles should be a relatively easy task.

It is best to display the completed puzzle in a spot where the entire congregation can see it.

The puzzle itself can picture a number of things. Some suggestions: denominational symbol and motto, line sketch of the church building and names of significant programs or activities, a welcome to students and teachers, a collection of Christian symbols with suitable scripture verse, a sketch of the earth with pictures/listings of outreach efforts. I have included a sample puzzle used for a six-class, fifty-person church school.]

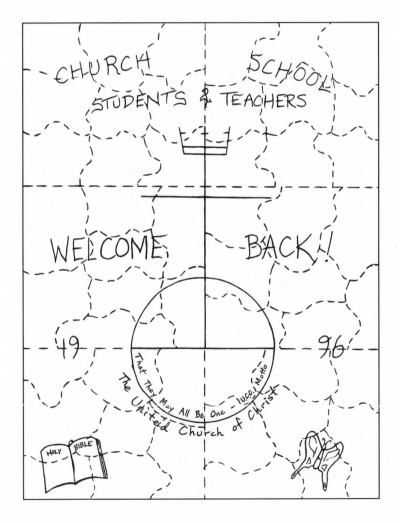

Reminders

Judaism

Materials: Several sticky-notes, a bill, a piece of string, a pack of gum, a mezuzah

There are all sorts of things in our lives that are important to remember. But often we have a hard time doing that. So we need things called *reminders* to keep us from forgetting what we ought to remember. I want to share a few different kinds of reminders with you.

1. Sometimes reminders are spoken words. These can be very direct: "Be sure to close the door when you come in from the snowstorm." Or they can be questions: "Do you think the peas and carrots are going to taste better when they're cold?" sort of reminds us we need to eat them.

2. Reminders can be written, too. These little sticky-notes from my desk remind me about people to see, places to visit, meetings to go to, stuff to do, bills to pay. [examine bill with wide eyes]

3. Some people use objects as reminders, objects such as this piece of string. They tie it around a finger and whenever they look at it, it reminds them of what they were thinking about when they put it there—or it reminds them that they're supposed to be remembering something they've already forgotten. (This is not really a very good reminder.)

4. Music is an excellent reminder. When you hear this [hum "Happy Birthday"], what does it remind you of? [responses]

5. Smells are terrific reminders, too. The smell of turkey often reminds us of what holidays? [responses] This smell [open pack

of gum] always reminds me of basketball or baseball because I chew gum when I play.

6. In places of worship like this church, we have all sorts of reminders around. The cross reminds us of Jesus' death and resurrection, the table reminds us of meals he shared with his followers. (Use other items, too—memorial plaques, stained glass windows, etc.)

Our Jewish friends have a particular reminder that they place by the doors of their homes. It is called a mezuzah. One kind of mezuzah looks like this. [show mezuzah] Inside it there is a little scroll to remind the people of the house that whether they are coming or going, they should love God with their whole hearts. In part, that is what the scroll says.

I think the idea of the mezuzah is a good one; sometimes we all need a reminder to love God. So I would like to suggest that we let the sun be like a mezuzah for us because it is at the entrance and exit of the day. It can remind us that whether the day is coming or going, or the night is coming or going, or we are coming or going, the most important thing to do is to love God and to love one another.

That's all the reminders I have, which reminds me—I'm finished!

Exodus

Passover

Materials: Eight signs containing the following words or phrases:
(1) Phewey! (2) Ribbet, ribbet, ribbet (3) There's a frog in my bed.
There are frogs in my cereal. (4) Buzz, buzz, buzz (5) Ouch, ouch, ouch
(6) Thud-thump, thud-thump (7) Munch, munch, chomp, chomp
(8) Hey! Who turned out the light?

Preparations: A person to play Pharaoh must be selected and told to
say "No!" each time the words "Pharaoh said ..." are used in the story.
Also, church school teachers or selected parents should be positioned
during the story so that they are between the gathered children and
the place the children will be going after the story (class, pews, fellowship room, etc.).

[*Note:* This story/dramatization is designed to teach about the
Exodus. It is particularly well suited as a lead-in to an explana-
tion of Passover by a Jewish guest.]

This is the story of a man named Moses, leader of the Hebrew
people, and of Pharaoh, the king of Egypt. I will narrate the story
and play the part of Moses. _____ (selected helper) will play
the part of Pharaoh. This is also the story of all those Hebrew
people who were kept as slaves by Pharaoh to make bricks for
him in his brickyard. All of you (the children) will play the part
of the Hebrew people. You will also be the sound effects crew for
the story by saying loudly the words on the signs I will hold up
at various times. Church school teachers, you are the Red Sea;
your part—pardon the pun—will come later.

Our story tells how Moses, with the help of his brother Aaron, listened to God's promise to set the Hebrew people free. It tells how he finally got to lead the people out of Egypt. It tells first of all how he had to deal with a very cruel and stubborn king.

As I said, the Hebrew people were slaves. Pharaoh refused to let them go. So Moses went to him and said: "Let my people go so they may worship God in the wilderness. If you don't," he went on, "my brother will touch the Nile River with his staff and turn it into blood." Pharaoh said, "No!" So Aaron used his staff and the river turned to blood. Fish died and it smelled horrible. [Show sign #1—Phewey!]

Moses again went to Pharaoh. He said, "Best let my people go to worship God in the wilderness. If you don't, Aaron will touch the ground and frogs will come out all over and be everywhere." Again, Pharaoh said, "No!" So Aaron touched the ground and there were frogs all over the place. [Show sign #2—Ribbet, ribbet, ribbet] It was disgusting. [Show sign #3—There's a frog in my bed. There are frogs in my cereal.] Finally, it got so bad that Pharaoh agreed to let the Hebrew people go. "Hooray," thought Moses. But when he got rid of the frogs, Pharaoh changed his mind and Pharaoh said, "No!" "Bah, humbug," thought Moses.

So he went to Pharaoh again and said, "Now look here. If you don't let us flee, I'll bring flies all over your land and people." Once more, Pharaoh said, "No!" So flies came all over and almost made the people wish the frogs were back to eat them up. [Show sign #4—Buzz, buzz, buzz] Finally, Pharaoh agreed to let the people go, but when Moses swatted all the flies out of the land, Pharaoh changed his mind and Pharaoh said, "No!"

All these terrible things, which are called plagues, kept happening because Pharaoh refused to let the Hebrew people go to worship God. While the plagues were happening, he would tell Moses that the people could leave, but as soon as the plagues stopped, over and over Pharaoh said, "No!"

There were plagues of terrible sores. [Show sign #5—Ouch, ouch, ouch] Plagues of hail. [Show sign #6—Thud-thump, thud-thump] Plagues of locusts. [Show sign #7—Munch, munch, chomp, chomp] Plagues of darkness. [Show sign #8—Hey! Who turned out the light?]

Finally, at last, there was one plague, one terrible thing, that made Pharaoh let the people go. (You can read about it in chapters 11 and 12 of the book of Exodus.) To this day, when our Jewish brothers and sisters celebrate the holiday of Passover, they remember this event of long ago, and they remember God's preserving the Hebrew people through trying and dangerous times.

By the way, it probably will not surprise you that after the Hebrew people left, Pharaoh changed his mind again and sent out his army to catch them. Trouble once more. Closer and closer the Egyptian army came, and there, right in front of the Hebrew people, was the Red Sea blocking their way. The army behind, the sea before them. But Moses raised up his hand, and the sea parted. [Teachers/parents divide their group to open a passage.] The Hebrew people got up and went through!

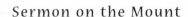

Sermon on the Mount

When Jesus told people about God, he usually taught them with little stories or sayings. But sometimes—at least one time—he gave what nowadays we would call a sermon. There is a particular sermon that Jesus gave which became very famous. It is called the Sermon on the Mount because Jesus spoke it to people who were gathered on a mountainside to hear him.

Since this is the only real sermon we have by Jesus, it is important for us to learn what it says. And in order to do that, we are going to play a game like one you have probably played before. This version is called "*Ser*mon Says." (It will help if you can stand up to play.)

Whenever I say, "Sermon Says," and then say something else while making a motion, I want you to make the same motion. That will mean that what I am saying is taken right from the Sermon on the Mount. But sometimes I will just speak and make a motion without saying, "Sermon Says." When I do that, don't do anything, because my words will not be from the Sermon on the Mount at all. I will just be trying to trick you. Let's try it!

Sermon says, blessed are the poor. [cup hands]

Sermon says, the realm of God is yours. [four fingers behind head to make a crown]

Sermon says, blessed are the hungry. [open mouth and point]

Sermon says, they shall be filled. [rub stomach]

Blessed are the rich and famous. [rub fingers greedily]

    Sermon doesn't say that!

Sermon says, blessed are those who weep. [rub eyes]

Sermon says, they shall laugh. [frame happy face with hands]

Do whatever you want. [hands extended, palms up, to the sides . . . shrug]

    Sermon doesn't say that!

Sermon says, blessed are those who are hated for my sake. [thumbs down]

Sermon says, they should jump with joy for God will reward them. [jump]

Hate your enemies. [snarl]

    Sermon doesn't say that!

Sermon says, love your enemies. [embrace]

Sermon says, treat others as you would like them to treat you. [extend hand as in handshake]

    Good job!

Bible

Materials: A used postage stamp, some already chewed bubble gum, an old and unbouncy tennis ball, an empty juice box, and two Bibles, one old and well-worn, the other one new

[*Note:* For use on a day when Bibles are presented to children.]

1. [Hold item] This is a postage stamp. As you can see, it has been used. It would be much more valuable if it were mint, that is, unused.

2. [Hold item] This is bubble gum. It has already been chewed. It would be much more appealing to us if it were unused.

3. [Hold item] This is a tennis ball. It has been whacked around hundreds of times. Since most of its bounce is gone, it is not much fun to play with. It would be much more lively if it were unused.

4. [Hold item] This is an empty juice box. Thirsty people prefer such a box to be unopened and unused.

[Hold up brand-new Bible]
This is a Bible that is brand-new, never opened, unused.
[Hold up old Bible]
This is a Bible I received a long time ago. It is sort of tattered and looks as though it has been used a lot. I hope that the Bibles we give out today end up looking like this old one, because a Bible is very different from the other things I showed you. Postage stamps, bubble gum, tennis balls, and juice boxes are more valuable, more interesting, more lively, and more nourishing when they are new and unused. But for a Bible to be valuable, interesting, lively, and nourishing to our faith (to us!), it just has to be used. The more you use it, the more it will be worth to you. So do use the Bibles—and check back in twenty years or so to see if they look like this old one.

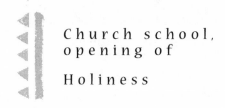

Materials: A doughnut, a pair of pants with several holes, a hose, an acoustic guitar

Since this is our first official children's lesson of the church school year, I wanted to make it especially good—thoughtful and inspiring and wise. So I decided to talk with you about what makes our faith holy and pleasing to God.

That is what I decided, but as soon as I started thinking about what to say, my mind began to do something your minds may do occasionally—it wandered. It went off in a direction I had not planned. You see, instead of thinking about holy things that have to do with our faith, it wandered into thoughts about other kinds of holey things, namely, things with holes in them. These turned out to be some of my favorite things, so I brought them along this morning.

The first is a food. [show doughnut] What is this? [responses] Right. It is a doughnut. Doughnuts are fun food. You can eat them many different ways: around the edge, by the piece, after dunking them in milk, and so on. And they usually taste great.

The second item is a pair of pants. [show pants] This is my favorite pair of pants. Besides the normal hole in the top to climb in and the holes in the bottom to stick feet through, it has a couple of others where it is worn and torn. This is the most comfortable pair of pants I own, and most often when I am wearing them I feel very relaxed.

The next item is a hose, which is sort of a hole in a long wrapper. I use one of these to water a garden or to wash a car or to fill a child's pool or to spray whoever's around. Every one of these activities accomplishes some useful work or allows some good fun.

The final item is a guitar. If this did not have a hole in it, the sounds made by the strings would just go "splat" against the wood, and whoever played the instrument could not share music with anyone very well at all. With a hole, the sound moves around inside and comes to life.

And now, guess what?! I believe my mind has wandered right back home. These four holey things just may tell us what it is that makes our faith holy and pleasing to God. You see, faith becomes holy when we get it inside of us for nourishment [hold up doughnut], when we wear it as easily as a pair of old pants [show pants], when we put it to use in our work and play [hold up hose], when we share it with others for the joy of it [show guitar; play a quick lick if possible].

Faith inside. Faith outside. Faith for each one of us. Faith for all together. That is the whole holy story.

Creation

Earthkeeping

Used July 2, '06

Materials: The three pictures provided; four index cards with the following words printed on them: (1) Earth, (2) Heart, (3) Earth Heart, (4) Hearth; a sheet of earthkeeping suggestions

[Hold up pictures in sequence. Wait for responses after questions.]

What does this picture show? [responses; then place "Earth" card by picture]

What does this picture show? [responses; then place "Heart" card by picture]

What does this picture show? [responses; then place "Earth Heart" card by picture]

I think all of us know that God gave us the earth as a home, and that God put a heart within us to give us life and feelings. This earth heart is a symbol that reminds us to have a heart for the earth, to care for it as God wants us to care for it. The symbol also reminds us that the earth has a life to preserve.

These are things we need to remember, and while I was writing out the words on the cards and drawing the pictures, I thought of an easy way to do that. Did you happen to notice that if you take the letter h from the end of the word "earth" and put it at the beginning, you get the word "heart"? And did you see that if you put the *h* at the beginning but also let it stay at the end, you get another word? This new word is "hearth." [show word on card] Does anyone know what a hearth is? [responses] A hearth is the place that used to be the heart of every house, the cooking place and gathering place for the family. The dictionary tells us it is the fireplace, but it tells us, too, that the word "hearth" can simply mean "home."

When we look at these pictures and scrambled letters with the eyes of faith, they offer us a single important message: To have a heart for the earth is to care for it as our home. Keeping that in mind, I want to give each of you a sheet that contains suggestions for taking care of this home God has given us, our earth.

[Hand out sheet of earth-keeping suggestions. This sheet should be created to suit local needs, circumstances, and opportunities.]

EARTH

HEART

EARTH
HEART

HEARTH

Diversity/Inclusiveness

Church

Materials: Three varieties of apples

Something I have always enjoyed doing is going to an orchard to pick a bag or basket of these. [show apples] What are they? [responses] Absolutely correct! I am sure you know lots about apples. But maybe you have never really considered what apples tell us about the church.

The way apples get gathered in reminds us of the way people get gathered together into a church congregation.

- Some are like apples on the ground; they need to be picked up in some way in order to join with the others.
- Some are like apples on the lower branches; just a welcoming hand will be enough.
- Some are like apples on the upper branches that have to be pulled down with a rake or a picking tool; they need a special kind of outreach.
- Some are like apples that can be shaken from a tree; if there is an open container, some of them will just drop in.

The different ways we eat apples tell us about the kinds of folks that God is glad to have in the church.

- Apple pies, apple crisp, or turnovers remind us that no matter whether people are crusty, crumby, or just plain flaky, they can be warm and good inside, and they are welcome here.
- Applesauce can help us remember that just as apples get squished to make it, some folks get feelings sort of

squished in their lives and so need the accepting love available at church.

- Caramel or candy apples let us know that in some ways we are all like the fruit inside the covering—a bit hidden to one another.
- Plain apples of many kinds, bruised or bright, remind us of all the colors, sizes and shapes of people who make up the church.

Probably cider, though, is the way apples tell us the most about the church, for we know that cider is at its very best when all sorts of apples get blended together into something tangy-sweet and delicious. The church is at its very best when it is a blend of all kinds of people brought together to serve God. When you see an apple, remember the church.

[Apples may be distributed to children.]

Faithfulness

Recycling

Materials: Glass jar, newspaper, T-shirt, aluminum can, picture of a plain cross

1. [Show glass jar] What is this? What do we do with it? (Among the probable answers: We eat or drink food or beverages that are contained in it. We store food in it. Sometimes we break it.)
2. [Show newspaper] What is this? What do we do with it? (Among the probable answers: We read it. We use it in the bottom of pet cages.)
3. [Show T-shirt] What is this? What do we do with it? (Among the probable answers: We wear it. We collect different kinds of T-shirts.)
4. [Show aluminum can] What is this? What do we do with it? (Among the probable answers: We drink from it. We save them to collect the deposit.)
5. [Show picture of cross] What is this? What do we do with it? (Among the probable answers: We use it as a symbol in our church. We learn about it. We may wear it.)

[*Note:* Point out that the cross is the most powerful symbol we have of God's love for all people.]

One more question for you. What can we do with *all* these things? [responses] I believe we can *recycle* all of them. It is quite obvious how we can do that with glass jars, newspapers, and aluminum cans. To recycle a T-shirt, we can donate it to a thrift store or use it as a craft material or a rag. Recycling all these items shows our love *for* God since it was God who created the earth and it is God who calls us to preserve it and to care for our brothers and sisters. But we can also recycle the love *of* God. We can do it each and every day, by paying attention to the teachings of Jesus, by passing along good deeds and kindness to persons in need, by trying to right what is wrong, and by returning love to others no matter how they treat us.

So—I invite you to be a recycler of your faith by letting the love of God be at the center of everything you do.

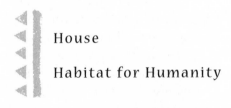

House

Habitat for Humanity

Way back when I was a child, I learned how important houses are. Nursery rhymes and fairy tales had much to say about houses. There was the crooked little man who lived in a crooked little house; there was a clever fellow named Jack who lived in the house that Jack built. Houses were made out of some pretty strange materials. The mean old witch that Hansel and Gretel met made a big house out of gingerbread and candy; an old woman who had more children than she knew what to do with had a shoe for a house. Everybody seemed to have a house—the giant with his mansion at the top of the beanstalk, Red Riding Hood's grandmother with her cottage in the woods, the three bears whose house Goldilocks messed up, and those three little pigs who had to deal with a one-wolf wrecking crew with a big bad appetite and a great pair of lungs. By the time I was ten years old, I was a homeowner. I spent hours and hours living in a tree house I had built in the backyard. [Adapt last two sentences to the presenter.]

Now that I am older, I still know that houses are very important to folks, and I have learned that many people do not have them. Today [or whenever a date is fixed] Habitat for Humanity is going to have a celebration here in _____ . It is called a groundbreaking, and what we are celebrating is the start of a house for a family who need one. This house is something that a large number of people will be helping to build (some in this church), and they will be doing that as a way of showing and sharing God's love for others. The house will *not* be made out of gingerbread, a shoe, straw, or sticks. It will *not* be a mansion. It will not be built by Jack alone but by dozens of folks. It will *not,* we hope, be crooked. It will *not* be up in a tree. But it will be built with lots of prayer and care and love, and with the great hope that many more Habitat houses can be built to become homes for individuals and families.

You are all invited to the groundbreaking. Come along!

[*Note:* This lesson can be modified to make it suitable for a house dedication.]

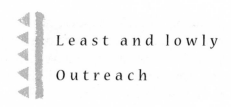

Least and lowly

Outreach

Materials: Penny, nickel, dime, quarter, half-dollar

When a friend of mine was in his late teens and early twenties, he worked at a small factory that produced and sold ice cream. One day, he and his co-worker Michael dumped ingredients into a big machine that would mix and freeze them. They put in gallons and gallons of milk and cream, huge bags of sugar, many pails of chocolate chips, three cups of green food coloring. A week or so after that batch was made, the factory's store started serving it in cones and dishes. People were not very happy. My friend's boss was not very happy. Michael and my friend had left out one ingredient that was least of all in terms of how much was supposed to be in the mix. Can you guess what that was? [responses] It was mint extract, less than a cupful. The store had many gallons of not very appealing green chocolate chip mintless mint ice cream. The *least* ingredient was the most important.

When we read aloud, we pay careful attention to all the shapes called punctuation marks. What are some of them? [responses] The *least* of the punctuation marks is the period, just a simple little dot. It does not seem like much until you try to read without paying attention to periods. I tried doing that with a children's book and found out that by page five I was so out of breath I could not continue. Those periods tell us when to stop, to pause, to start a new idea, to take a breath. They are very important.

I have brought five coins with me—a penny, a nickel, a dime, a quarter, and a half-dollar. The dime is the *least* of these in size. It is worth more than two of the other coins and less than two.

85

Now for a puzzle. Suppose someone were to say to you, "I'm going to fill a shoebox with one kind of coin and then give it to you." If you wanted to receive the most amount of money, which coin would you choose to fill up the shoebox? [responses] You would receive the most if you chose the dime. It may be the least in size, but for the space it takes up, it is the most valuable.

Sometimes we think of certain folks as the "least" of people in the world. The homeless. The mentally retarded. The very young or the very old. The hungry who live far away. The lonely who live next door. Prisoners. Kids no one seems to like. We may try to leave them out of our lives or think they are not worth much. What Jesus had to say about these folks, though, is that they *are* important and valuable. To God and to us. In fact, he told his followers that how we treat the "least" is actually how we treat *him*. What that means for us is that we need to be as loving and caring to everyone as we would be if Jesus were right here in front of us. And do you know what? When we do care and love in that way, Jesus *is* right here—not in front of us, but inside us and among us.

Church

Ecumenism

Materials: The shoes described in the text

How is the church like feet?

That is a strange question, but I believe that in a few minutes we will have some ideas about how to answer it.

I have brought with me a box that contains some shoes and boots. Let me show them to you. We have several kinds here.

Tennis shoes or basketball shoes—These are tough yet comforting and shock-absorbing.

Slippers—These are light and lined so they are warm and cozy.

Rubber-soled boots—These are made for tromping through slush or swampy ground, for walking in muck or mud.

Dress shoes—These are for special events or for occasions that are somewhat fancy and formal.

Old boots or moccasins—These are for knocking around while doing errands or light work outside.

Jogging shoes—These are designed for being active and on the run, for getting somewhere quickly.

These shoes serve different purposes, yet they are all useful and valuable to my feet.

One of the questions I get asked a great deal is why the Christian church is divided up into all sorts of denominations, Methodists and Lutherans and Roman Catholics and Baptists and Disciples and Pentecostals and many more. Folks say, "Shouldn't there be just one church?" And I have started to answer this way . . .

I say: Think of the church as like your feet, moving about trying to do God's will on earth. And think of all the denominations as different kinds of shoes that help the church do all it needs to do. There really is only one church (just as God gives us, at most, one pair of feet), but the shoes we call denominations enable the church to have a whole variety of appearances and functions. Some denominations have a toughness about them, while others have a softness and warmth; some get right into muddy issues, and others emphasize beauty and formality; some have a relaxed feel, and others try to keep always in motion and on the go.

Feet need all sorts of shoes to do what they can do. The church needs a variety of denominations to accomplish all that it can in the world. Our hope is that we can learn to work together, to share our soles—and our souls—with one another, so that we can serve God well.

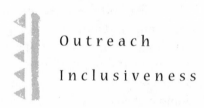

Outreach

Inclusiveness

Materials: An empty bag and a bag full of empty cans and bottles

One of my hobbies is walking. Perhaps I have waved to you when you passed by in a car or on a bicycle. One of my other hobbies is something I do when I am out taking a walk. This particular hobby requires very simple equipment: a bag [show one] and a pair of these [show hands]. I call this hobby "pickin' up empties." On a good day I will come home with something like this [show full bag].

Years ago, I used to pick up empties now and then to throw away. They were as useless as any other trash along the roadside, and when I tossed them into a garbage pail I did so only to help clean up the environment. Then folks began to realize that aluminum and glass could and should be used again and again, that old cans and bottles could be made into new cans and bottles. So each was given a value—usually a nickel or a dime—and my hobby took on a whole new meaning. I began to look at empties differently and I began to look harder for them, to reach out for them more eagerly. I became aware that the cans and bottles by the roadside were not useless throwaways; they were redeemable and they had worth.

In a way, some of the work of the church is very much like my hobby of "pickin' up empties." Among us and around us, here and all over the world, there are people whose lives have a certain emptiness to them: they are empty with loneliness; they are empty because they have lost the hope that once filled them; they are empty from some kind of loss. There are many folks who have empty pockets and empty stomachs. And lots of people who might help out just walk on by. *But* here in the church, we are reminded that these "empty people" have a value that God gave to them; we are taught that reaching out to them is part of our mission; and we are urged to notice that outreach picks us up, too, as we recognize the value of others.

All of what I have said gets around to the One Great Hour of Sharing. (Other mission giving projects and programs may be substituted here.) This collection is one of the best ways we have of "pickin' up empties," of putting our hand out to people who are empty in one way or another. It is a way of filling their needs for tools or food or medicine or knowledge or hope or love.

When you see cans or bottles by the roadside, you can pick them up or you can leave them for me. But please do not pass by those people near and far who need our help. They are sisters and brothers to Christ and to us. They are valuable in the sight of God.

Gifts

Diversity

Did you bring your gifts with you this morning?

This is a bit of a trick question. Most of us, when we think of a gift, assume that it has to be something we buy, something we can see and touch. But there are other kinds of gifts as well. Let me give three examples of gifts other people had that they shared with me. All these people were classmates of mine in elementary school or junior high.

The first person was named Elizabeth. When I was in fourth grade I went to her house to play because none of my usual friends were home and my mother had to go out. I was not at all thrilled to be at Elizabeth's house, mainly because I liked running around and she was in a wheelchair. But I found out that day that Elizabeth had an incredible gift for drawing. She helped me see things differently so I could draw better myself. That is the gift she gave me. We used up half of a thick pad of paper that afternoon, and I remember whining when my mother came to pick me up, "Do I have to go already?"

The second person became a friend in about eighth grade. When I visited his home, he showed me all sorts of objects from Africa—masks, drums, pictures, water pitchers, a spear. He told me his family had long ago been brought here from Africa as slaves, so all the things his family collected helped him remember where his ancestors had come from. This friend's name was Rashon, and in his living room there was a huge black piano. I asked if anyone in his family played it, and that is when Rashon shared his gift with me. He sat down and played a song called "Watermelon Man," and then a couple of other pieces. The music was jazz and blues. It was as different from the music my parents played as the masks were different from the watercolors on our wall at home. I loved the music. And then Rashon told me about jazz and blues musicians with wonderfully unusual names: Thelonius Monk and Jelly Roll Morton. Rashon had an astounding gift for piano-playing. He shared that with me and gave me my love for a whole new kind of music.

The third person was named Stephen. I got to know him in sixth grade. Before I went to his house for the first time, my parents said, "Don't be asking about where the toys are or what there might be to eat. Stephen's family doesn't have much." When I got to the house, I realized that Stephen's family really was poor. But he had a ball, so we played catch for a long time. And he had a shovel, so we built a fort. It was not until we went into Stephen's room that I realized what a wonderful gift he had—he had an amazing imagination. His room was full of neat toys, all things he had made. He had assembled them out of wood, pieces of metal, rope, all sorts of materials. That afternoon we put together a terrific baseball game. And the gift I got from Stephen was a trust in my own imagination.

All the gifts I have mentioned are ones that came to my friends from God, and the gifts came to me from my friends. I believe that all of you have special gifts—things you do well and talents you can share. I hope you will use your gifts and share them with others. God wants us to do that giving and sharing.

[*Note*: These examples may be used as written, may be attributed to a friend, or may be experienced as memory aids enabling the reader to recall similar incidents from his or her past.]

Homelessness

Mission

Materials: Six pictures—a bird's nest, a mouse hole, an igloo, a house or apartment building, a car, a large box

I am going to show you some pictures in a minute, and I would like you to tell me what they are. Then I am going to ask a second question about each one. Ready?

[Show picture of bird's nest]   What is this?   [responses]
                                     Who lives in this?   [responses]

[Show picture of mouse hole]   What is this?   [responses]
                                     Who lives in this?   [responses]

[Show picture of igloo]   What is this?   [responses]
                                     Who lives in this?   [responses]

[Show picture of house   What is this?   [responses]
 or apartment building]   Who lives in this?   [responses]

[Show picture of car]   What is this?   [responses]
                                     Who lives in this?   [responses]
                                     (Children may respond that no one
                                     lives in a car. Address this response
                                     after showing and hearing responses
                                     to the next picture.)

[Show picture of large box]   What is this?   [responses]
                                     Who lives in this?   [responses]

Sad to say, people sometimes find themselves living in a car or a box, or having no place at all as a home.

When we look at pictures and talk about homes of different kinds, I hope we think thankfully about how good it is to have a place to live. And I hope, if we find ourselves blessed with such a place, that we imagine what it feels like to be without a home . . . to be homeless.

Cars, boxes, and no place are no places for people to live. With God's help and our effort, we can try to create a world where the homeless are not hopeless, where they can come to have places that they can call their own.

[*Note:* This lesson might continue with a description of any church activities supporting or staffing shelters, funding soup kitchens, advocating for the homeless, or creating housing. A possible introduction: "It is extremely difficult when you are homeless, having no single place to live, to know who you neighbors are. What Christian people must try to do is say through their actions: 'We are your neighbors. And we see that *you* are our neighbors in need of help. So, however we can, we will.' "]

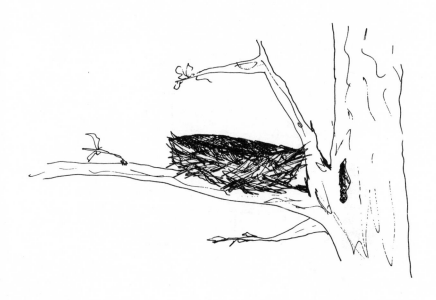

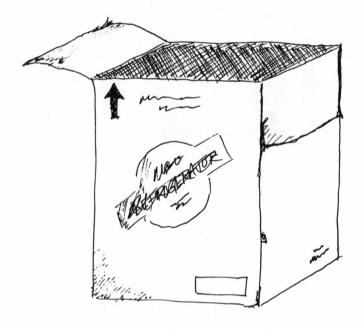

Mission

[*Note:* This piece, though structured for use in a congregational context, may be modified for an all-children setting by having participants divide into two lines that will turn to face one another during the "statue-forming" portion of the exercise.]

It takes a good deal of practice to become skilled as an actor or actress. But the practice is often fun. One of the exercises sometimes used by drama teachers is having students listen to a word, then become a statue that shows what the word means. Today you are going to have an opportunity to do this. I will give an illustration. [Use a word such as "surprise" or "sneakiness" as inspiration for the demonstration statue.]

Please stand up and face me. Let's see how you do as actors. Here is a practice word; try to form yourself into a statue that shows the meaning of the word "happiness." [statues take form]

Great job! Now, let's show everyone how talented you are. When I say a word, I would like you to act out the meaning of that word by becoming a statue of its meaning. Really let me see the word in you. Then, when I believe you have it just right, I will say, "Turn around," and when you do that, everyone will see.

The first word: Fear	Turn around!	[turn back]
The second word: Hunger	Turn around!	[turn back]
The third word: Hopelessness	(imagine that nothing good is happening to you)	
	Turn around!	[turn back]
The fourth word: Anger	Turn around!	[turn back]

Excellent! Have a seat again.

These words we have acted out are feeling words. Now that we have seen them and maybe felt them, try to think what it would be like to have your friends or family or yourselves feel the meaning of these words all the time.

There are people throughout the world who have these feelings every day. They live in fear because of violence all around them. They know the constant hurt of hunger. They feel a hopelessness brought on by ongoing illness or poverty. They ache with an anger at those who make promises to them that are not kept.

It is these people—real people, not statues—that Jesus tells us to treat as brothers and sisters. It is these people that the church is called to care for most of all. We try.

[Words on mission programs might follow.]

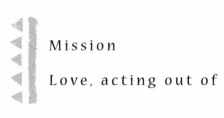

Mission

Love, acting out of

Materials: Large envelopes with the following postal markings
(by rubber stamp or sticker) and the described contents

	Marking	Contents
#1	Priority Mail	A pocket Bible
#2	Fragile	Pictures of refugees and victims of malnutrition
#3	Special Delivery	A seed packet, a picture of food, an adhesive bandage, a sock
#4	Return Receipt	A letter from a foreign country (from someone involved in church work, if possible)
#5	Spoiled	—

As you may know, the word "mission" means "to be sent." I started thinking last week about those things that get sent more than anything else—letters. And as I thought, it occurred to me that the different kinds of markings on letter envelopes can serve to remind us about different parts of our Christian mission activity. Let's take a look.

#1   This envelope is marked "Priority Mail." The priority, the first thing, for persons involved in mission work is to extend the love of Christ to others. The source for learning about that love is the Bible [show pocket Bible], and if we truly go "by the book," it will lead us to a number of creative ways of sharing love. Of sending ourselves. Let's look at the other envelopes.

Bible passage   99

#2 This envelope is marked "Fragile." The lives of many persons in this world are extremely fragile. They are broken by war or hunger or disease. [show pictures] To send our love means sending people skilled in building peace, growing food, healing illness, teaching, and training.

#3 This envelope is marked "Special Delivery." When there is disaster, severe need, or ongoing shortages, then special deliveries are in order. So sending our love may mean shipments of [show items] seeds, food, clothing, medicine.

#4 This envelope is marked "Return Receipt." To be involved with mission work means keeping in touch with those who receive what we send. It is important to remember that those we intend to help have much to teach us; what they return [show letter] is their gift to us. Loving means listening.

#5 The final envelope is marked "Spoiled." It has nothing inside; it is absolutely empty. So it is that our mission efforts get spoiled when we are empty inside, when we send no support, no love, nothing of ourselves.

Jesus taught throughout his life that the love of God is connected with a love for persons in need. For people in the church, we must always be working together to figure out ways of sending and delivering that love, of being people with a mission.

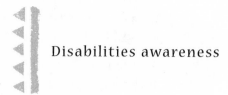

Disabilities awareness

Materials: A tightly sealed jar, a dime, a blindfold

If I were to tell you that someone was disabled, what would that mean? [responses]

There are millions of people in this country who are in some way disabled, and one of the things the whole church is trying to do is to understand better what it is like to be disabled. Only when we understand can we best welcome and involve persons who are disabled in the life of the church. This morning I am going to give a few of you the opportunity to feel, for a couple of minutes, the challenge of having a disability.

[Select four persons.]

#1 Your situation is that you have one arm. [give sealed jar] Your task is to open this jar and then to seal it again.

#2 You are to be someone who is blind. [cover eyes with blindfold] Your task is to pick up a dime that has fallen to the floor. [place dime 10–12 feet from the searcher]

#3 You are someone who cannot hear. Please go halfway back in the church and then follow the instructions I give you. [Allow time. Then mouth the following statement without making any sound: "I want you to come back here right away." Repeat several times. Finally, gesture for the person to come back.]

#4 Your situation is that you are unable to speak. I want you to find out some information from anyone in the congregation. Please come listen to your instructions. [Whisper these instructions: "Without making a sound, your task is to find out how much the Sunday newspaper costs."]

What did it feel like to have a disability? [responses]
[*Note:* It should be pointed out in discussion that sometimes enabling devices are needed, that great ingenuity and special skills may be required, that having things in their proper place takes on a high degree of importance. Children might observe feelings of being different or separate from others, of needing more time to do certain tasks. Emphasize the aspect of overcoming challenges and becoming adaptable.]

Those who are disabled develop ways of accomplishing tasks that are different from our ways; often they need to exercise an admirable creativity. They have a great deal to teach us about dealing with challenges. What we try to do in the church is to get past seeing persons with disabilities as different (We are all different from one another!) and to make sure we welcome them and their gifts. We want to hear their special needs as well as receive their talents; we want to focus on abilities more than disabilities; we want to give access to every person for every activity of church life. Perhaps by taking part in today's lesson you will better understand the challenge of disabilities and will become enthusiastic welcomers of persons with disabilities into our church family.

Index